UNITED NATIONS CONFERENCE ON TRADE AND DEVELOPMENT
GENEVA

TRADE AND DEVELOPMENT REPORT, 2000

Report by the secretariat of the
United Nations Conference on Trade and Development

UNITED NATIONS
New York and Geneva, 2000

Note

- Symbols of United Nations documents are composed of capital letters combined with figures. Mention of such a symbol indicates a reference to a United Nations document.

- The designations employed and the presentation of the material in this publication do not imply the expression of any opinion whatsoever on the part of the Secretariat of the United Nations concerning the legal status of any country, territory, city or area, or of its authorities, or concerning the delimitation of its frontiers or boundaries.

- Material in this publication may be freely quoted or reprinted, but acknowledgement is requested, together with a reference to the document number. A copy of the publication containing the quotation or reprint should be sent to the UNCTAD secretariat.

UNCTAD/TDR/(2000)

NOTICE TO READERS

New schedule of publication

This is the last edition of the *Trade and Development Report* to be issued in the autumn. Publication will henceforth be in the spring of each year, beginning in April 2001.

FOREWORD

UNCTAD's *Trade and Development Report* has become a valuable analytical source on trends and prospects in the global economy, and its challenging analysis of pressing economic issues is eagerly anticipated, particularly by policy makers in the developing world. This year's *Report* continues the tradition. Fortunately, the economic storm clouds which began gathering over East Asia in 1997 have now broken, and the world economy last year posted a recovery that surpassed expectations. However, even as the digital age creates new opportunities, financial fragilities in the world economy continue to constrain policy makers everywhere. Given the severity of East Asia's financial crisis, much of the focus and concern in recent years has been on developments in the region. This year's *Report* takes a careful look at the forces driving the recovery in East Asia, its weaknesses and the longer-term prospects and policy options for sustained growth and development.

Kofi A. Annan
Secretary-General of the United Nations

Contents

Chapter I

THE CURRENT GLOBAL RECOVERY AND IMBALANCES IN A LONGER-TERM PERSPECTIVE

Chapter II

List of text tables and charts

List of boxes

Explanatory notes

Classification by country or commodity group

The classification of countries in this Report has been adopted solely for the purposes of statistical or analytical convenience and does not necessarily imply any judgement concerning the stage of development of a particular country or area.

The major country groupings distinguished are:

» Developed or industrial(ized) countries: in general the countries members of OECD (other than the Czech Republic, Hungary, Mexico, the Republic of Korea and Turkey).

» Transition economies: the countries of Central and Eastern Europe (including the States formerly constituent republics of Yugoslavia), the Commonwealth of Independent States (CIS) and the Baltic States.

» Developing countries: all countries, territories or areas not specified above.

The term "country" refers, as appropriate, also to territories or areas.

References to "Latin America" in the text or tables include the Caribbean countries unless otherwise indicated.

Unless otherwise stated, the classification by commodity group used in this Report follows generally that employed in the UNCTAD *Handbook of International Trade and Development Statistics 1996/1997.*[1]

Other notes

References in the text to *TDR* are to the *Trade and Development Report* (of a particular year). For example, *TDR 1999* refers to *Trade and Development Report, 1999* (United Nations publication, sales no. E.99.II.D.1).

The term "dollar" ($) refers to United States dollars, unless otherwise stated.

The term "billion" signifies 1,000 million.

The term "tons" refers to metric tons.

Annual rates of growth and change refer to compound rates.

Exports are valued FOB and imports CIF, unless otherwise specified.

Use of a dash (–) between dates representing years, e.g. 1988–1990, signifies the full period involved, including the initial and final years.

An oblique stroke (/) between two years, e.g. 1990/91, signifies a fiscal or crop year.

Two dots (..) indicate that the data are not available, or are not separately reported.

A dash (-) or a zero (0) indicates that the amount is nil or negligible.

A dot (.) indicates that the item is not applicable.

A plus sign (+) before a figure indicates an increase; a minus sign (-) before a figure indicates a decrease.

Details and percentages do not necessarily add to totals because of rounding.

---

[1]   United Nations publication, sales no. E/F.98.II.D.16.

Abbreviations

ACP	African, Caribbean and Pacific (group of States)
ASEAN	Association of South-East Asian Nations
BIS	Bank for International Settlements
bpd	barrels per day
CEPAL	Economic Commission for Latin America and the Caribbean (Comisión Económica para América Latina y el Caribe)
CFA	Communauté financière africaine (franc zone)
CIS	Commonwealth of Independent States
CIF	cost, insurance and freight
ECA	Economic Commission for Africa
ECB	European Central Bank
ECE	Economic Commission for Europe
ECLAC	Economic Commission for Latin America and the Caribbean
EMS	European Monetary System
EMU	Economic and Monetary Union
ESCAP	Economic and Social Commission for Asia and the Pacific
EU	European Union
FAO	Food and Agriculture Organization of the United Nations
FDI	foreign direct investment
FOB	free on board
GATT	General Agreement on Tariffs and Trade
GDP	gross domestic product
GNP	gross national product
HIPC	heavily indebted poor country
HPAEs	highly-performing Asian economies
ICT	information and communications technology
IIF	Institute for International Finance
ILO	International Labour Organisation
IMF	International Monetary Fund
IPOs	initial public offerings
IT	information technology
LDC	least developed country
MERCOSUR	Southern Common Market (Mercado Común del Sur)
MFN	most favoured nation
NAFTA	North American Free Trade Agreement
NIEs	newly industrializing economies
NPLs	non-performing loans

ODA	official development assistance
OECD	Organisation for Economic Cooperation and Development
OPEC	Organization of the Petroleum Exporting Countries
SOEs	state-owned enterprises
SSA	sub-Saharan Africa
TFP	total factor productivity
TNCs	transnational corporations
UNCTAD	United Nations Conference on Trade and Development
UN/DESA	United Nations Department of Economic and Social Affairs
UNDP	United Nations Development Programme
UNU	United Nations University
WIDER	World Institute for Development Economics Research
WTO	World Trade Organization

OVERVIEW

Two big global economic forces are competing for the world's attention. On the one hand, the promise of a "new economy" underpinned by information and communication technologies is exciting policy makers, including those from the world's poorest countries. On the other hand, growing instability and uncertainty linked to globalization has left them deeply worried about the impact of financial shocks on growth prospects; the experience of some of the most successful developing countries has shown just how virulent those forces can be.

So far the big winner has been the United States. On some accounts the spread of new technologies has already uplifted its growth potential. But financial crises in emerging markets have also helped to sustain rapid growth in the United States as capital was attracted to this safe haven and cheap imports helped keep the lid on inflation. By contrast, the impact of new technologies has been much less evident in Europe and Japan. As regards developing countries, most of their firms have had little or no benefit so far, and this digital divide is of growing concern to policy makers.

Disparities in growth rates within the industrial world and a strong dollar have resulted in growing trade imbalances as the United States has become "buyer of last resort" to the world economy. At the same time, the combination of technological and financial innovations has aggravated the underlying fragility of current financial and trade flows. The mania for cross-border mergers and acquisitions has contributed to a larger worldwide financial bubble in technology stocks, whose prices have been rising much faster than productivity, even in the United States.

The task of adjustment to global economic imbalances is falling on monetary policy alone. This is a cause for concern. Current global macroeconomic imbalances bear some disturbing resemblances to those of the 1970s and 1980s, when the absence of cooperation and coordination among the major economic powers led to systemic breakdown and hard landings. And what we have learnt about the global economy over the past few decades tells us that failure to resolve such imbalances in an orderly manner will be most damaging to growth in the developing countries.

Global economic growth and imbalances

The world economy made a welcome turnaround in 1999, confounding fears that it would drop into recession. Robust growth was also accompanied by an improvement in world trade and the return of some degree of normalcy to currency and financial markets, after the chaotic conditions of the previous two years. This was greatly helped by a combination of unexpected and one-off events.

The expected chaos from the Y2K computer bug and the associated economic costs proved grossly exaggerated; in the event, the business expenditure undertaken worldwide to avoid any potential disruption provided a massive shot in the arm for the world economy, estimated at some 1–2 per cent of global GDP. The reversal of policies of austerity in East Asia in the second half of 1998 helped to repair much of the earlier damage to output from the financial collapse, and pushed growth in the developing world ahead of that in the industrial countries after the shortfall in 1998. Sharply increased oil prices gave an unexpected boost to the Russian economy, allowing it to register a moderate growth against widespread expectations of deepened recession.

But above all, the United States economy continued to surge ahead, belying forecasts and growing well above what was customarily believed to be the longer-term potential. With economic growth exceeding 4 per cent, unemployment dipping below 4 per cent, and imports rising by 12 per cent, the United States economy continued its role as white knight to the global economy.

All in all, the immediate prospects for the world economy have improved, with growth this year expected to exceed 3 per cent. Considerable encouragement can also be taken from the way the world has shrugged off the sharp rise in oil prices since mid-1999. The impact on inflation has so far been negligible, and simulations undertaken by various organizations suggest that the effect of continued high oil prices on global growth will be limited and confined mostly to oil-importing developing countries.

It is also possible that the world economy will become even more robust over the coming years, with a consolidation of global growth accompanied by increased stability. The United States economy may become neither too hot nor too cold, engineering an orderly slowdown to a sustainable growth rate compatible with the greater potential arising from new technologies. Stronger growth in Europe and Japan, propelled by adaptation to the new economy, would relieve the United States of its role as the sole engine of global growth. In this ideal scenario oil prices and interest rates will level off and the dollar will gradually be realigned so as to consolidate price and financial stability. And renewed private capital flows, together with continued domestic reforms and the spread of new technologies, will begin to deliver the promised fruits of globalization to developing countries.

However, there is also a recognition that the wreckage from the Asian crisis will not be cleared away by simple incantations to the new economy, and that making good on the promises of globalization will call for considerable policy effort. Not only are the root causes that led to the fear of recession during 1998–1999 still present, but also further fault lines have emerged, along which any unexpected movements could have damaging consequences not only for industrial economies but also, and of greater concern, for developing countries. Prospects for the latter could deteriorate rapidly if the major industrial countries continue to set their policies without regard to their global repercussions on trade and capital flows.

The factors that have helped the United States economy to surge ahead have also increased financial fragility and global imbalances. The flight of capital to quality that started after the Asian crisis, and accelerated rapidly in autumn 1998 following that of the Russian Federation, provided an important stimulus to the United States economy by accentuating the bubble in asset prices and thereby encouraging private spending based on capital gains. The combination of rapid growth in domestic demand and a strong dollar has also resulted in mounting external deficits, reaching 4 per cent of GDP. The recovery in emerging markets has added to demand for dollar assets as reserves are piled up as a safeguard against future crises. Japan, like other surplus countries, is also willing to hold its trade surpluses with the United States in the form of dollar assets. The coincidence of a budget deficit and rising supply of government bonds in that country with a budget surplus and falling supply of government bonds in the United States has held out the prospects of gains on United States government bond holdings, triggering a flow of funds from Japan. European and Japanese TNCs have joined in the process of buying into the technological gains already made by United States firms. Headline-grabbing mergers and acquisitions in the high-tech sector have spilled over into a financial bubble in technology stocks, where self-fulfilling expectations rather than solid earning prospects have been moving the market.

A combination of dwindling private savings, rising private debt, mounting current-account deficits and the bubble in technology stocks, whilst providing a Keynesian fillip to the United States economy, has been sustained by the continuing attractiveness of dollar-denominated assets to non-residents. But this situation cannot continue indefinitely. The factors accelerating growth in the United States have also reduced the effectiveness of monetary policy in engineering a soft landing; higher interest rates have so far served to attract more capital from abroad, thereby fuelling asset prices and adding to effective demand, the strength of the dollar, and the trade deficit.

By contrast, in 1999 growth in EU failed to match that of 1998, but is generally expected to reach or exceed 3 per cent this year, harbouring hopes that EU will soon replace the United States as the global growth engine. However, even under a scenario of accelerated growth, Europe is unlikely to provide a comparable demand stimulus to the rest of the world. Its growth spurts have been dependent on exports, helped last year by a weak euro and the strength of the United States economy. The tensions inside Euroland between fast- and slow-growth economies complicate considerably the search for a common monetary stance at a time when the policy autonomy of the European Central Bank (ECB) has been compromised as a result of closer integration of global financial markets, the increased responsiveness of capital flows to interest rates in the United States and, contrary to original expectations, the consolidation of the dollar's status as a reserve currency. Any hike in United States rates could check investment spending and derail growth in Europe. None of this points to an accommodating macroeconomic stance that could underpin a high-tech Keynesian recovery of the kind enjoyed in the world's richest economy in the past few years. Nor is the situation helped by the hypnotic hold which the notion of a non-accelerating-inflation rate of unemployment (NAIRU) still has over European macroeconomic policy, even though the theory that high unemployment rates are structural and cannot be brought down without accelerating inflation is now discredited by the experience of the United States, where expansionary policies fuelled productivity growth.

The economy of Japan picked up last year after contracting by over 2 per cent in 1998. However, strong first-half growth figures in 1999 owed much to extra government spending, and the annual growth rate was dragged back down to a mere 0.3 per cent as this injection of funds petered out. The East Asian recovery did help thanks largely to the presence of Japanese producers in the region, and now that private expenditure appears to be picking up, prospects are more encouraging, pointing to a growth rate perhaps in excess of 2 per cent for the year as a whole. Still, private spending remains structurally constrained by the financial legacy of overinvestment during the boom years of the late 1980s and by the creeping rise in unemployment, which is now close to 5 per cent. The confidence of Japanese households and firms remains brittle, and finding the right course is complicated by mounting public debt, now standing at over 100 per cent of GDP. Japanese policy makers would do well to recall that the United States deficit was tackled in the context of accelerated growth. Recovery in Japan is also vulnerable to a premature tightening of monetary policy and a strengthening of the yen.

The experience of the 1960s and 1980s shows that large imbalances in external payments and capital flows between the United States and other major industrial countries can pose serious threats to global growth and stability, since the willingness of investors in surplus countries to hold dollar-denominated assets can come to an abrupt end. That these imbalances are now associated with deficits of the private, rather than of the public, sector makes the situation all the more fragile in view of the greater risk involved in holding private liabilities.

While a rise in United States interest rates relative to the rest of the world does little to reduce global imbalances in growth and trade, it is in any event unlikely to occur, since ECB tends to track United States interest rates in an effort to defend the new currency, while emerging markets are obliged to follow suit in order to retain capital inflows. A generalized rise in interest rates in the industrial world, including Japan, which now looks set to abandon its policy of zero rates, would do little to alter the current pattern of exchange rates and trade balances, but would create problems for debtor developing countries. Since fiscal tools are no longer in the armoury of macroeconomic management and policy coordination comes, if at all, with crisis management rather than crisis prevention, an orderly adjustment of imbalances without sacrificing growth may be too much to expect.

Thus, as in previous episodes, the danger is that a policy impasse will end with much more abrupt changes than are either needed or desirable. Such an outcome would be of grave concern to developing countries, since their economic fundamentals are hyper-sensitive to movements in foreign interest rates and capital flows, and their exports would be seriously affected by the slowdown in growth.

The vulnerability of developing countries to policy shifts in the major industrial countries will, of course, depend on their current state of health. Conditions in Latin America deteriorated further in 1999, with a contraction in GDP per capita for the first time since 1990. Growing trade deficits and falling capital inflows throughout the region were signs of a continent in trouble. However, there were some sharp differences among countries. Mexico posted a relatively strong performance, thanks to its increasingly close ties to the United States, as did some smaller countries in Central America and the Caribbean. Elsewhere, weak commodity prices and the collapse of intraregional trade meant that policy-making was carried out in an unfavourable environment. But the heavy-handed policy response to the threat of financial contagion, including fiscal tightening and high interest rates, tipped some countries into recession. Things could have been much worse for the region if Brazil had not weathered its financial storm surprisingly well. By contrast, Argentina's defence of its dollar peg took a much heavier toll on its real economy last year, with output dropping by over 3 per cent. For the region as a whole the basic policy challenge remains how to break free from an excessive dependence on external resources.

The economies of developing Asia turned strongly upwards in 1999, growing on average by more than 5 per cent. The big economies of India and China continued to sustain their above-average performance, but it was the sharp recovery in East Asia which attracted most attention. The rebound in the Republic of Korea has been spectacular, and Malaysian growth reached double-digit figures in the first months of 2000. The revival became evident in the first half of 1999 and owed much to expansionary monetary and fiscal policies, and a further fillip was provided by exports, which began to reap the advantages of currency devaluations. The high degree of regional integration was a critical ingredient: the collapse of intraregional trade was a major conduit of contagion, and recovery has been amplified through the same channels. While balanced growth is expected in 2000, there remain downside risks for some countries, such as Indonesia.

China also benefited from the regional recovery in 1999, but its 7 per cent growth was still the slowest in a decade. Short-term easing of monetary and fiscal policies to boost demand failed to stimulate private consumption, leaving exports and government expenditure to underpin growth. With rising fears of unemployment, consumer confidence seems unlikely to improve, and policy makers are looking for a new growth path which could break the forces of deflation, over-production and excess capacity. Accession to WTO is expected to contribute, but greater emphasis is also being placed on developing the internal regions. On the other hand, if accession to WTO necessitates a devaluation of its currency to protect some of the country's less competitive industrial enterprises (particularly those still under state ownership) against an unexpected surge in imports, other countries of the region are likely to be affected in consequence. Indian growth was based on the dynamism of industry and services. Even with a sharp slowdown in agriculture, the economy expanded by close to 7 per cent in 1999, and the growth momentum is expected to continue this year.

Africa was again unable in 1999 to match the growth peak of 1996. Indeed, with growth dipping even below the 3 per cent achieved in the previous two years, per capita income actually stagnated. There were nonetheless some bright spots. The CFA countries benefited from the depreciation of the euro in 1999, which boosted their competitiveness and a combination of political stability, agricultural growth and increased capital inflows in North and East Africa produced some encouraging performances. After a number of lean years, the economies of Nigeria and South Africa appear to have bottomed out. But on the whole, neither the domestic nor the external conditions are yet right for an African growth revival. In many countries, political conflicts and the weather left economic policy makers with few options. Elsewhere, the vagaries of global commodity markets took their toll. Weak prices for beverages and a sharp downturn in cocoa and coffee prices were particularly damaging, and oil-importing countries have been badly hit by the hike in prices. Growth may accelerate moderately in 2000 if commodity prices strengthen, albeit with gains heavily concentrated in North Africa. But for sub-Saharan Africa the basic policy challenge remains how to overcome savings and foreign-exchange constraints and to raise investment to hit at least 6 per cent growth per annum. This will need increased official financing and debt relief along with a more pragmatic approach to domestic reforms.

The transition economies posted their highest growth in a decade, some 2.4 per cent. But volatility and variation are endemic to the region. Contagion from the Russian crisis dominated developments in the first half of the year. However, marked improvements in exports to EU allowed many countries in Central Europe to grow faster than the regional average. More surprising still was the recovery in the Russian Federation, where growth in 1999 ended up at over 3 per cent thanks to the sharp rise in oil prices and the devaluation of the rouble. The momentum is expected to be sustained this year. Nevertheless, weak export performance and lingering fears of inflation in the transition economies continue in many cases to create difficulties in obtaining international finance. Despite the ending of open conflict in South-East Europe, the macroeconomic situation there remains fragile and economic prospects bleak. The challenges for these countries are not unlike those in much of the developing world, and again the response of the developed countries has so far been insufficient.

* * *

Despite a rapid recovery from the depressed conditions of 1998, external vulnerability is still a looming menace to growth prospects in the developing world. Concerted efforts by developing countries to become full participants in an increasingly interdependent global economy continue to be stymied by biases and asymmetries in the trading and financial system. There are too many exporters struggling to gain access to the markets of the rich countries, and the kind of extreme price movements previously suffered by commodity producers have also begun to upset the plans of manufacturers. A reluctance to move towards a new round of multilateral trade negotiations that took into consideration the development needs of poorer countries, including the problems they confront in implementing commitments in the Uruguay Round, was apparent in Seattle, and the trade imbalances among major industrial countries simply adds to the anxieties of the developing world. Even after years of hard-won domestic reforms, developing countries are still dependent on highly volatile capital flows to support growth.

Growth prospects of developing countries will depend on how these concerns are addressed. In an increasingly interdependent global financial and trading system, it is clear that trust in market forces and monetary policy alone will not carry the day. Increased international cooperation and dialogue will be needed if the full potential of new technologies to bridge the growing gap between the rich and poor is to be realized. This calls for much bolder leadership, of the kind which heralded in the last Golden Age.

Crisis and recovery in East Asia

The potential damage to developing countries from the combined influence of global imbalances and speculative pressures was brutally exposed by the financial crisis in East Asia. The speed of recovery in the region over the past year has been encouraging. However, the fact that neither the depth of crisis nor the speed of recovery was anticipated even by those responsible for policy should caution against excessive exuberance.

Although the crisis in each country had its own characteristics, there is little doubt that the extremes of collapse and recovery have, in large part, been due to misguided policies. The initial policy response was unnecessarily severe and the expectation that tight monetary policies would quickly stabilize the currency, resulting in an investment-led recovery, was misplaced. Monetary tightening aggravated the crisis by deepening the debt deflation process set off by speculative attacks, and served to depress output and employment. Nor were currencies stabilized as a result of the hike in interest rates; that outcome came rather from the build-up of reserves due to massive cuts in imports, and from reductions in foreign claims due to debt rescheduling or to more unorthodox measures, such as capital controls. Indeed, the hike in interest rates proved to be much more damaging than currency depreciations, causing serious dislocations in the corporate and financial sectors.

The economies only bounced back when policies of austerity were reversed and governments were allowed to play a more positive role. The policy reversal was brought about by the depth of the crisis and by widespread criticisms rather than as part of a carefully sequenced policy package; in this respect, the positive influence on the entire region of the example of Malaysia in pursuing policies based on autonomously set objectives and priorities cannot be emphasized strongly enough. In retrospect, provision of adequate international liquidity to replenish reserves, accompanied by temporary exchange controls and a debt standstill and roll-over (measures recommended by the UNCTAD secretariat early in the crisis) would have been a much more effective response than the policy of high interest rates actually followed.

With the exception of Indonesia, per capita incomes have returned to or exceeded pre-crisis levels; exchange rates have strengthened; interest-rate spreads in international borrowing have narrowed significantly; and foreign capital has begun to return. However, there are reasons for concern. In the first place, recovery has been accompanied by only limited corporate restructuring, and the health of the financial system continues to rely on public intervention in the credit mechanism.

Second, exports are unlikely to continue at their recent pace, and public deficits and debt have been on the rise in most countries seriously hit by the crisis. Since premature fiscal tightening could stifle growth, fiscal consolidation needs to wait until private demand takes the lead in growth. But this process may be delayed because of persistent unemployment and the existence of excess capacity in many branches of industry.

Finally, the recovery has so far been supported by highly favourable conditions in the world economy which are susceptible to change. A sharp slowdown in the United States and a deterioration in global financial conditions could be particularly damaging, since already external payments in the region are moving towards deficits, enhancing the need for external financing. Hikes in foreign interest rates could pose a dilemma: attracting foreign capital would call for a reversal of the easy monetary stance, but that could stifle growth by blocking the domestic forces of recovery and aggravating the difficulties of the banking system.

As in other episodes of financial crisis in emerging markets, shifts in macroeconomic aggregates, notably the decline in the domestic resource gap and the improvement in the current-account balance, as well as sharp currency devaluations, have been associated with significant adverse changes in income distribution in East Asia. Employment and wages have generally lagged behind aggregate income in the recovery, and poverty has remained considerably above pre-crisis levels. This is consistent with a troubling pattern in the developing world, where the poverty-alleviating impact of a recovery in growth is significantly weaker than the poverty-augmenting impact of a comparable decline.

The longer-term implications of all this for the East Asian economies are far from clear. If growth in the region is adversely affected by unfavourable global conditions, then the malign social legacies of the crisis will persist for some time. Only with a more inclusive growth pattern, at rates closer to the longer-term average, can the fight against poverty be effectively resumed. How governments manage to withdraw from the business of crisis management and get back into the business of managing integration into the world economy will be crucial.

A fundamental lesson of the financial crisis is surely that excessive reliance on foreign resources and markets leaves growth prospects vulnerable to external shocks. Policy makers have rightly rejected a retreat into protectionism, but it would be just as wrong to allow global market forces to dictate future growth and development. With domestic savings likely to remain high, dependence on foreign capital to close the income gap with the leading industrial nations will be that much less. Greater attention also needs to be given to domestic sources of growth, such as rising wage shares and higher social spending. There is a major role for public investment and the involvement of a developmental State, with new policy agendas. Regional economic ties are likely to remain important and should be strengthened, *inter alia*, through collective defence mechanisms against systemic financial instability and contagion.

Rubens Ricupero
Secretary-General of UNCTAD

THE CURRENT GLOBAL RECOVERY AND IMBALANCES IN A LONGER-TERM PERSPECTIVE

A. Growth and imbalances

Recovery and sustained growth in the global economy has been subject to two challenges since the 1997 Asian crisis, one being on the real side and the other involving the financial sector. The first threat was the impact on developed economies of the expected sharp increase in competitiveness and exports from East Asia as the crisis-stricken economies benefited from massive currency devaluations, requiring large swings in trade balances. The second threat was that of a global collapse of financial markets as a result of the rush to liquidity following the Russian debt default in late summer 1998. Both developments gave rise to widespread forecasts of a global slowdown and concerns over a risk of recession.

In the event, neither of these threats materialized and the global economy appears to be enjoying sustained expansion. The threat from a deluge of exports from East Asian countries in that period was largely offset by the collapse of their financing systems and asset prices, as a result of which the initial adjustment was based not on increased exports but on massive cuts in imports. Even when exports increased in volume, the effect on earnings was more than offset by falling export prices, while the decline in imports of primary materials compounded a downward trend in world commodity prices that had already started

in 1996. The net result was an increase in the purchasing power of consumers in developed countries that allowed demand and output to expand rapidly in conditions of price stability.

In the absence of price pressures, the United States Federal Reserve allowed the economy to grow at a rate exceeding by far what it considered to be the potentially non-inflationary level, thus enhancing the productive potential and the rate of non-inflationary growth. Growth continued at rates that were not only above forecasts but, at more than 4 per cent, double of what was considered as the maximum potential. Indeed, the potential growth rate has now been revised upward, from around 2.5 per cent to more than 3 per cent, in view of what appears to be a stable annual increase in labour productivity to rates above 2 per cent.[1]

The consequences of the fall in primary commodity prices were especially acute in the Russian Federation, where tax receipts and foreign exchange earnings had become almost totally dependent on commodity trade. The decline in export revenues led to the default on interest payments on government debt and a collapse of the rouble. Since many developed-country financial institutions were exposed either directly or indirectly, the insolvency of the Russian Government threatened global financial stability; there was a loss of confidence in all but the most secure financial investments, and the funding of all but highly secure government paper dried up. United States government securities thus became the refuge of risk-averse investors and commanded a large liquidity premium.

In this instance the Federal Reserve not only refrained from raising interest rates, but also acted quickly to reduce them to counter the rising risk premium and the sale of financial assets, thereby averting the threat to global growth of the contagion implicit in the linkages between national financial markets. This monetary easing, which was extended into 2000 through efforts to counter the risks of a systemic breakdown that was feared on account of the "Y2K computer bug", did much to allow the United States economy to continue to function as the engine of world growth, in particular by providing markets for the recovering East Asian economies. In the second half of 1998 those countries had already started to benefit from accommodating domestic fiscal and monetary policies and had finally unleashed the export potential implicit in their large devaluations and excess capacity, producing record current-account surpluses.

Thus, the factors that countered the two threats to the global economy during 1998–1999 have served to accelerate growth in the United States. They also led to a sustained inflow of capital into that country in excess of its current-account deficits, as international investors sought the security of dollar assets. The attractiveness of the dollar, together with the concentration of new issues of internet technology companies in the United States, helped to produce a sustained increase in asset prices that has provided the basis for increases in both private investment and private consumption expenditures. Rapid growth and a rising dollar have resulted in a growing current-account deficit as the United States acted as "buyer of last resort" from the rest of the world. This combination of a rising current-account deficit and a strong dollar is reminiscent of the early 1980s, when it was widely considered to be unsustainable and was the source of the "hard landing" of the dollar in 1986–1987.

As in the 1980s, the Japanese surplus has been the major counterpart to the United States deficits, but now there are substantial differences that serve to reinforce the current imbalances. The first and most obvious is that the United States growth differential vis-à-vis the rest of the world is now underpinned by private spending and productivity gains due to a new Schumpeterian technological epoch, and the government is a net saver. In Japan, growth is negligible and the attempt to combat falling prices and stagnant private spending is creating rising government deficits and debt. As a result, the supply of United States government bonds that serve to satisfy the increased global preference for dollar assets is declining, while the supply of Japanese government bonds, which do not, is increasing. In such conditions the natural result is for rates on United States bonds to fall and on Japanese bonds to rise, creating expectations of gains on the former and losses on the latter. Such expectations have largely offset the recent attractiveness of Japanese equities to foreign buyers and supported the flow of funds from Japan to the United States. Since Japanese financial institutions hold a large proportion of domestic bonds, any substantial increase in domestic interest rates will lead to large capital losses, impede the process of reconstruction of the financial system and reduce lending to the private sector.[2]

The East Asian crisis and recovery have also reinforced the demand for dollar assets. The current-account surpluses generated in the region are seen as necessary not only to provide the funds to repay the short-term dollar debt, but also to satisfy the increased liquidity preferences of these countries in the form of larger international reserves as a buffer against future crises. Thus, the claims on the United States generated by its trade surpluses are willingly held as dollar assets to provide a defensive liquidity cushion. High United States interest rates favour the holding of reserves in dollars, the more so in view of the large losses sustained on holdings in the newly issued euro assets. Reserves are further supplemented as countries intervene to sell their currencies against the dollar to prevent unwanted real appreciations which might choke off the recovery process.

Thus the East Asian region, which has the world's largest export surplus, through its tendency to hold those surpluses in dollar assets, has provided support for the dollar but made it difficult for the United States to reduce its deficits. As the recovery continues, imports will rise and current-account surpluses will shrink, but capital flows to the region are likely to increase. Since the volatility of capital flows was the major reason for the earlier crisis, it is likely that these countries will continue to hold larger proportions of their capital inflows as reserves, maintaining the increased demand for dollar assets as risk and liquidity hedges.[3]

Europe is the other major region with a current-account surplus. Growth in EU has in general not been sufficient to bring about reductions in unemployment, although there are some important exceptions. Europe has lagged behind the United States in the exploitation of new technologies in communications and computing to increase productivity. Consequently, there are now substantial differences between labour productivity growth in Europe and the United States, constituting a reversal of the post-war trend for European productivity to dominate. One way to overcome this lag has been to acquire United States companies or to start up operations in the United States; indeed, the United States has become a net recipient of FDI. While European FDI flows to that country more than tripled from 1995 to 1998, reaching more than $160 billion, the flow in the opposite direction rose from $50 billion to $70 billion.[4] Since many United States firms are now truly global corporations, they are considered as global investments, and European portfolios have increased their holdings of United States equities. This process was given a further boost by the introduction of the euro, which eliminated the benefits from diversification of assets denominated in other EU currencies.

Neither the strength of the dollar vis-à-vis the euro nor higher United States interest rates has done much to reduce current imbalances in trade, growth and capital flows between Europe and United States. Since the strong dollar is due to foreign demand for dollar assets, it supports consumption in the United States by feeding through to household wealth, given the relatively high share of equity in household portfolios, as well as by increasing purchasing power. Thus, high interest rates are not very effective in preventing overheating through their effect on domestic demand and the dollar. On the other hand, since in EU trade with the rest of the world is a small proportion of GDP, one can expect little expenditure switching from the United States to Europe as a result of the weakness of the euro. By contrast, to the extent that the strong dollar induces the European Central Bank (ECB) to raise interest rates, domestic sources of growth may be dampened and

the restructuring of the EU slowed. It thus appears that the strength of the dollar exacerbates the differential in demand growth between EU and the United States.

Persistence of similar imbalances between the United States and Europe in the 1960s contributed to the breakdown of the Bretton Woods system. At that time the dollar was weak in the presence of large outflows from the United States on account of non-commercial transfers linked to political and military objectives. These flows were accompanied by a persistent budget deficit, a positive growth differential and a negative interest differential with Europe. The United States wished to avoid using higher interest rates in support of the dollar in order not to slow growth, and the weakness of the dollar made little contribution to the correction of external imbalances. There was no agreement on whether the appropriate policy was the reduction of the United States' budget deficit and growth or an increase in European demand and growth. Unwilling and unable to act on exchange rates, the United States introduced a wide variety of capital controls. The impasse was eventually resolved by abandoning the Bretton Woods system and taking the dollar off gold.

In the current situation, the equivalent fiscal measure to reduce United States trade deficits would be an increase in its budget surplus. While this might have been the policy response in the era of Keynesian fine-tuning of the 1950s and 1960s, it is no longer considered desirable; nor is the use of expansionary fiscal policy considered desirable by EU in the light of the Stability and Growth Pact. Thus, the entire burden of adjustment is placed on monetary policy, i.e. a rise in interest rates in the United States relative to those in EU. But, if such adjustment simply increases the attractiveness of dollar assets and further feeds the bubble in equity prices, it may become self-defeating. The increased role of the dollar as a reserve currency and the closer integration of global capital markets thus constrain the effectiveness of United States monetary policy in cooling the economy and reducing its trade deficits. What might be required in the present context is a reverse interest equalization tax to reduce the return to non-residents on their holdings of United States assets.[5]

In any case, adjustment in global imbalances through a relative rise in United States interest rates is unlikely since most emerging markets need to follow suit in order to retain capital inflows. More fundamentally, ECB has started to increase interest rates in an attempt to ward off anticipated inflationary pressure, even though growth in EU is barely 3 per cent and the decline of the euro has hardly affected prices. It is clearly unwilling to follow the Federal Reserve lead in attempting to discover if potential growth rates could be raised by a more accommodating policy.

A parallel increase in both United States and European interest rates (and an eventual increase in Japanese rates to convince corporations to restructure rather than carry losses at zero interest rates) would have little impact on exchange rates of the currencies of the countries concerned or on trade imbalances, but it would sharply increase the carrying costs of debt in developing countries. Increasingly, developing country economic fundamentals, such as fiscal and current-account balances and the inflation rate, are dependent on foreign interest rates. In some economies (e.g. Argentina and Hong Kong, China) this link is more direct, whereas in others (e.g. Brazil and many East Asian countries) it operates through the external debt burden and capital flows. In all cases, however, higher international interest rates would pose a serious threat to the recovery in emerging markets. In East Asia, where recovery has taken place without any substantial corporate and financial restructuring, higher interest rates will simply make this process more onerous, and the recovery may eventually be stalled by the failure of the domestic financial system to provide finance.

A strong European recovery, which has been expected since 1993, has been repeatedly retarded by rising United States rates because increased integration of financial markets and attempts by ECB to establish credibility have resulted in rising interest rates in Europe also. It is unlikely that growth could accelerate in Europe in the face of a United States downturn accompanied by a slowdown in Latin America and East Asia. Thus,

the risks that were identified in the aftermath of the Asian crisis continue to be present.

As noted above, similar unsustainable imbalances were present in the global economy for substantial periods in both the 1960s and the 1980s, before creating serious disruptions in global growth and dampening the prospects of developing countries. In the past, excess savings of the rest of the world were balanced by excess spending by the United States Government, and the demand for United States assets was met by the issue of government securities. Today, it is the United States private sector that is sustaining global spending. Since the government is running a fiscal surplus, the demand for dollar assets due to increased uncertainty over global asset values cannot be met by increasing the supply of risk-free United States government securities but would require the issue of assets by the private sector. The basic question is whether foreign investors seeking liquidity and safety will be equally willing to hold private assets. As long as internet stocks dominate investor attention, large expected gains can offset their risk spread over government securities, and the dollar can become the transaction currency for international equity trading. This tendency will be reinforced by the fact that the integration of Europe's largest equity markets is taking place between London and Frankfurt, thus providing little support to the euro. Further, the movement towards listing many developing-country companies in New York financial markets to ensure sufficient liquidity simply reinforces the tendency for the dollar to become the vehicle currency in the global equity market. Nonetheless, since private debt is not a perfect substitute for Treasury debt, the increasing United States budget surplus can add to the fragility of the current situation and raise the possibility of a "hard landing" for the dollar. In such an event global prospects will depend very much on how monetary policy is conducted and coordinated among the United States, Europe and Japan.

B. Eliminating global imbalances and sustaining growth

Whenever large global imbalances are built up by self-sustaining processes, such as those currently prevailing, uncertainty increases. Current uncertainties, however, are not over the nature of future events, but rather over their timing and implications. There can be little doubt that growth in the United States economy will slow, either of its own accord or induced by continued action on interest rates by the Federal Reserve. By the same token it is certain that the trade deficit will in time be reduced.

It is also likely that the European recovery will be choked off because of a fall in exports as the United States economy slows autonomously, or because the Federal Reserve increases interest rates and ECB mirrors those increases. Consequently, although its economy is equivalent in size to that of the United States, EU is unlikely to take over the role of the United States in supporting global demand. Growth in EU is unlikely to be much above 3 per cent on the basis of domestic demand, and even if it did manage to replicate United States growth rates, it would not generate an external deficit similar in size to that of the United States. Thus, EU cannot replace the United States as the global "buyer of last resort" for the recovering Asian and Latin American economies.

Now that imports in East Asia have recovered to more normal levels, any slowdown in the world economy would once again worsen the external accounts in those countries and render them more dependent on capital inflows. Most countries in the region have built up massive dollar reserves to meet this contingency and they may soon have to use them. Tighter balance-of-payments constraints will bring growth rates back to lower levels. Before the Asian crisis, the region accounted for roughly one half of the annual growth in global demand, and it is unlikely to return to this position, at least in the foreseeable future.

Just as in Europe, Japan has been unable to generate growth based on private domestic expenditure, on the model of the United States, and growth remains dependent on exports. The East Asian recovery has provided a beneficial complement to its fiscal expenditure programmes, but now that growth in East Asia is constrained, recovery in Japan will not be particularly robust, and at any rate too weak to offset the slowdown in the rest of the world, particularly in the United States.

Latin America also depends on global markets. Indeed, outward-looking development strategies in many of these countries depend for their success on mutually reinforcing regional and global growth. A slowdown in United States growth would consequently adversely affect the Latin America economies also.

It is thus evident that optimistic forecasts of a return to global growth at rates above 3 per cent make an implicit assumption about how the decline in United States demand will be compensated for internationally. Obviously, the optimal scenario would be that of a natural decline in United States growth without any further increases in interest rates in either the United States or Europe. If tight monetary policy has to be used to quell the United States' expansion and is also applied in Europe, eventually accompanied by Japan's abandonment of its zero interest rate policy, then indebted developing countries will be doubly burdened by falling export receipts and higher financing costs. If higher interest rates produce financial market turmoil, such as occurred in the global bond market in 1994, which produced losses in net wealth far in excess of the 1987 stock market crash or the Asian crisis, then developing countries could also find themselves severely restricted in their access to private finance. Clearly, a collapse in bond prices would quickly be transmitted to equity prices, which could substantially reduce United States growth as consumers cut back on their expenditures to meet rising interest and margin payments or adjust to their lower wealth levels. In 1994 high interest rates were accompanied by a decline in the dollar. Normally, such a decline would be beneficial to developing countries. However, if a global financial market turmoil produced a massive shift to liquid assets, it is likely that, as in 1998, the dollar would become the currency of refuge, producing a combination of high interest rates and a strong dollar that was so detrimental to indebted developing countries in the 1980s. While the distribution of financial indebtedness in the present situation is different, and fewer liabilities are held in variable rate form linked to the United States interest rate, a number of countries have direct linkages, either through currency boards or through indexing of debt, allowing a quick and direct transmission of deflationary forces to their economies.

Thus, the prospects for the world economy are not as optimistic as the surprising recovery in 1999 has led many to believe. This much is clear: the remnants of the wreckage of the Asian crisis of 1997 cannot be swept away by another East Asian "miracle" or by the new technologies that appear to be shifting the United States onto a higher potential growth path. An increasingly interdependent global financial and trading system can scarcely function efficiently with only one policy tool, monetary policy, especially without appropriate coordination. The restoration of fiscal policy to the armoury of defensive measures, as well as increased international cooperation, will be required if the full potential of new technologies is to be realized and set the world economy on a higher growth path, thereby enabling developing countries also to achieve sustained increases in per capita income. ■

Notes

1   Already in 1995 the UNCTAD secretariat argued that low estimates of potential growth and high estimates of natural rates of unemployment were due to hysteresis, and that industrial economies could grow much faster without an acceleration in inflation and could reduce unemployment to levels below the estimates of natural rates if appropriate policies were pursued (*TDR 1995*, Part Three, chap. III). See also *Newsweek*, 18 Sept. 1995: 38–39.

2   Around 40 per cent of the existing stock of government bonds is held by government agencies such as the Trust Fund Bureau. About a quarter is in bank portfolios. It has been estimated that a 100 basis point rise in interest rates on long bonds in February 1999 would have produced a capital loss of 1.5 trillion yen for bank holders alone. See IBJ Securities, Economic analysis report: The dual managed system of the moratorium period, *IBJS Research & Reports*, April/May 1999 (www.ibjs.co.jp).

3   On the increased tendency to accumulate excess reserves in emerging markets see *TDR 1999*, chap. V.

4   UNCTAD, FDI/TNC database.

5   Similar measures were used in the past, for instance by Switzerland in the early 1970s, when negative interest was paid on deposits by non-residents to slow capital inflows.

Chapter II

THE WORLD ECONOMY: PERFORMANCE AND PROSPECTS

A. Introduction

In contrast to the turbulence of the previous year, 1999 was characterized by a stabilization of global economic conditions and a revival of world production and trade. The widely anticipated major disruptions, and even the threat of global recession, arising from the "Y2K computer bug", turned out to be, in effect, a non-event. Although the risk itself may have been exaggerated, the absence of serious disruptions is perhaps a reflection of the massive business spending undertaken to cope with the problem. While there are no reliable figures, the most widely quoted amounts for such expenditure on global information technology (IT) range from $300 billion to $600 billion,[1] which is some 1–2 cent of global GDP. It appears to have provided an important boost to the world economy, giving an additional stimulus to the United States and helping recovery in East Asia.

World GDP growth picked up significantly in 1999, to reach 2.7 per cent, having slowed to 1.8 per cent in 1998 from 3.4 per cent in 1997 (table 2.1). Of particular significance is the turnaround from recession to growth in Japan and the transition economies as well as the recovery in developing countries. The major factor underlying faster growth in developing countries as a whole was a steep rebound in East Asia, which more than compensated for a mild slowdown in Africa and a more severe one in Latin America. As a consequence, overall growth in developing countries was once again higher than that of developed countries, for the second time since 1988.

In 1999, output of the United States continued to maintain its expansion at a pace faster than 4 per cent. Its sustained import demand was the main driving force behind the improvement in the global economy and particularly in Asia and Europe. Following recession in 1998, the Japanese economy rebounded sharply in the first half of 1999 but slowed again later in the year. Growth in EU was significantly lower in 1999 than in 1998 but developments during the year were positive. Despite increased monetary and financial convergence, growth rates continued to diverge considerably among EU countries.

Prospects are for a slowdown in the United States, but whether it will be an orderly transition to more moderate and sustainable growth rates or take the form of a "hard landing" is still an open question. The Japanese economy is expected to strengthen unless there is a premature tightening of monetary and fiscal policy or a sharp appreciation of the yen. Growth in Europe is likely to exceed the 1999 rate unless it is cut short by rising United States interest rates. Prospects in the developing and transition economies depend very much on what happens in the industrial world. Under the consensus forecast, growth in these economies should, on average, be stronger and more evenly distributed among countries. However, there is also the risk of a double squeeze: on the financial side, through rising interest costs of external finance and falling capital inflows; and, on the real side, through falling export earnings.

Table 2.1

WORLD OUTPUT, 1990–1999

(Percentage change over previous year)

Region/country	1990–1995[a]	1996	1997	1998	1999[b]
World	2.1	3.5	3.4	1.8	2.7
Industrialized economies	1.8	3.1	2.9	2.0	2.5
of which:					
United States	2.5	3.6	4.2	4.3	4.2
Japan	1.4	5.0	1.6	-2.5	0.3
European Union	1.6	1.6	2.5	2.7	2.3
of which:					
Germany	2.0	0.8	1.5	2.2	1.5
France	1.1	1.1	2.0	3.4	2.7
Italy	1.3	1.1	1.8	1.5	1.4
United Kingdom	1.6	2.6	3.5	2.2	2.0
Transition economies	-6.9	-0.1	2.2	-0.6	2.4
Developing economies	4.9	5.7	5.5	1.3	3.4
of which:					
Africa	1.3	5.2	3.0	3.0	2.7
Latin America	3.6	3.6	5.3	1.9	0.1
Asia	6.1	6.8	5.9	0.9	5.1
of which:					
China	12.0	9.6	8.8	7.8	7.1
Other economies	4.9	6.1	5.1	-1.0	4.4
Memo item:					
Developing economies, excluding China	4.1	5.1	5.0	0.3	2.8

Source: UNCTAD secretariat calculations, based on data in 1995 dollars.
　a Annual average.
　b Estimated.

B. Developed countries

1. United States

The United States economy continued to defy forecasters and economic theorists in 1999. Consensus forecasts were for growth to slow to some 2.5 per cent, which was widely considered as the highest sustainable rate consistent with price stability. While the 2.8 per cent growth in the first half of the year suggested that the forecasts might

prove correct, the rapid acceleration in the second half, to an annualized 6.5 per cent, strongly influenced by business investment in IT, and large liquidity injections by the Federal Reserve to insure against a Y2K breakdown of the payments system, produced the third consecutive year of growth in excess of 4 per cent, with falling unemployment having no appreciable impact on inflation. By the end of the year the economy was growing at a rate well above 5 per cent with no signs of deceleration in the first quarter of 2000, driving unemployment below 4 per cent for the first time since the 1950s.

The acceleration of the economy in the second half of 1999 led the Federal Reserve to reverse the policy of interest rate cuts that had been used to combat the global liquidity crisis in the fall of 1998, and to resume in August the process of monetary tightening "in small steps" that it had started in 1997. The target Federal Funds Rate was raised from 5 per cent to 6 per cent in 25 basis-point increments, before a 50 basis-point increase took it to 6.5 per cent in May 2000. In addition, the reversal of the large injections of liquidity to insure against a Y2K breakdown have further tightened monetary conditions. Although productivity and labour force growth have continued above historical trends, the Federal Reserve is concerned that the supply response to the rapid growth in demand may be insufficient to prevent the emergence of inflationary pressures. In addition, recovery in Europe, East Asia and Latin America adds to the pressure on world prices, most clearly reflected in the rise in oil prices.

The United States expansion, now the longest in post-war history, is a textbook case of one driven by private spending sufficiently high to produce constantly falling unemployment and a rising fiscal surplus in conditions of price stability. However, there are a number of aspects which suggest that growth at present rates is unsustainable and will eventually be reduced, either directly through monetary policy or by the reaction of markets to the increasing financial and trade imbalances in the economy.

The role of the United States as global "buyer of last resort" after the East Asian crisis has raised its current-account deficit from less than 2 per cent of GDP in 1997 to nearly 4 per cent in 1999. In 1998 earnings on net external assets turned negative and the figure more than doubled in 1999, adding to the rising trade deficits. The deterioration in the external balance is aggravated by the strength of the dollar, which has served to reduce the dollar value of foreign exchange earnings (since over 50 per cent of United States claims are on Europe and the euro had depreciated by some 20 per cent against the dollar in 1999), and by return differentials in favour of dollar assets. Irrespective of the financing of its trade deficit, the United States has now to borrow every year to meet the servicing of its net foreign liabilities.

Private spending, which had been financed largely by internally generated funds at the beginning of the recovery, is now financed by borrowing by both households and business. The private sector savings ratio has reached historical lows and household saving has been negative in some months. This also suggests that some private-sector borrowing is undertaken to meet interest payments.

Finally, as in the past, sustained expansion has been accompanied by buoyant asset markets which create a fertile climate for financial excess. The last United States expansion, in the 1980s, produced the bubble in real estate prices due to excessive lending by savings and loan associations, which led to a collapse of the thrift industry,[2] and many argue that the recent rise in equity prices has been excessively rapid and represents a bubble based on self-fulfilling expectations rather than solid earnings prospects. It thus represents similar risks of a dramatic collapse. Returns to investors in equity markets have been driven by the rapid improvements in the quotations of initial public offerings (IPOs) of companies utilizing the new information and communications technology (ICT), but which often have no record or expectation of positive earnings. One analyst has described this process as equivalent to Keynes' recommendation for a depression cure based on burying money in bottles and allowing people to dig it up: internet IPOs are "a newly elegant flip on Keynesianism: pay people to start companies that never make money, but that spread a lot of money around to others in the meantime".[3] The success of these new issues has had beneficial effects on traditional sectors such as automobiles, real estate and business-related services. The collapse of this source of financing would thus have serious ramifications for the entire economy.

The ability of the United States economy to sustain expansion is clearly linked to its ability to sustain its borrowing to finance the current-account deficit, its negative private savings, and the creation of new business enterprises through the new issues market. But, as is usual in periods of sustained expansion, lending goes increasingly to projects whose success depends on the expansion being sustained. This gives rise to financial instability and financial distress when the expansion comes to its inevitable end.

The recovery in East Asia and Europe suggests that there should be some relief in this precarious pattern for the financing of the current-account balance. The dollar has declined from its peaks of late 1998, so United States exports should benefit from both higher foreign demand and increased competitiveness. However, the consequent improvement in net exports will not help the Federal Reserve in slowing domestic demand growth, although it should reduce the risks of a sharp decline in the dollar and panic sales of dollar assets that would lead to an equity market collapse. While increasing interest rates may also lend support to the dollar, it is important to recall that the last round of tightening by the Federal Reserve in 1994 led to dollar weakness rather than strength.

Since private spending is clearly linked to lending, the United States economy may be returning to the model of the 1960s, when monetary policy worked by increasing borrowing costs to the construction sector and quickly reduced new construction and employment. Now the link between monetary policy and economic activity is provided mainly by start-up business in ICT, which is highly dependent on continued financing either from banks or from the stock market. Thus, the rise in interest rates and its dampening impact on the stock market will eventually cause business expenditure to slow. The question is whether the result will be a sharp decline, leading to a recession, or whether there will be a "soft-landing" whereby the growth rate stabilizes at around 3 per cent.

The first signs that the economy might be slowing started to emerge in the spring of 2000, when retail sales, durable goods orders, new housing starts and new mortgage applications all declined, and unemployment claims rose. The unemployment rate rose back above 4 per cent and average hours worked fell. Household consumption grew by less than household income, leading to a reversal of the decline in the savings ratio. As always, the resumption of interest rate increases by the Federal Reserve has heightened uncertainty about asset prices, and stock market volatility has grown sharply with price variations in the Nasdaq index, as measured by the standard deviation of daily returns exceeding 5 per cent in April. The index, which covers most of the new internet and technology companies, fell by nearly 40 per cent in three months, from March to May 2000, while the Dow Jones industrial average has been virtually unchanged over the same period, suggesting substantial capital losses to households and a sharp reversal of the bubble that was pro-

viding much of business and household financing. So far the dollar has not come under heavy pressure in this period of substantial market losses in sectors that have been of greatest interest to foreign investors.

2. Japan

Japan has been struggling to emerge from a prolonged recession that has been plaguing the economy since the collapse of the equity and property market bubble at the beginning of the past decade. Expectations of a sustainable recovery took hold in 1999 as the Japanese equity market finally showed signs of a recovery at the end of 1998, climbing by around 25 per cent in the course of 1999. This was accompanied by a recovery of the yen, which appreciated from more than 140 yen to the dollar in the summer of 1998 to around 100 yen by the end of 1999. Much of the demand for Japanese equities came from foreign buyers, with United States investors accounting for 60 per cent of total foreign purchases of some 11,000 billion yen in 1999, compared to 2,000 billion yen in 1998. There was also a sharp reversal in other forms of capital flows, from a net outflow to a net inflow. This was mainly due to the disappearance of the yen premium, which had previously resulted in lending by Japanese parent banks to their overseas branches, and in the use of swaps by foreign banks operating in Japan. Repayment of these loans, the unwinding of swaps and repatriation of capital due to closures of many of the overseas branches of Japanese banks combined to produce what must be considered a one-off reversal in capital flows.

The expectation of recovery was less dominant in Japan itself, and private spending remained stagnant, while growth was driven by government expenditures and exports. Quarterly GDP growth rates, which had been in the range of 3–5 per cent in the first half of the year, seemed to indicate a turnaround, but negative growth at similar rates in the second half left the result for 1999 as a whole at 0.3 per cent. The contribution of public investment, which had accounted for around half of GDP growth in the first half, turned negative in the second half, as did the contribution of private expenditure.

At an annual rate of 10 per cent, the preliminary GDP growth figures for the first quarter of

2000 show an even stronger start to the year than in 1999, pushing the growth for the whole fiscal year towards the government target of 0.6 per cent. This is the highest quarterly increase since the first quarter of 1996. At the time, the performance for the first quarter did not prove to be sustainable, so caution may be needed in interpreting the current figures, but the industrial production data, which are considered to provide a more accurate gauge of the state of the economy, and operating ratios for the manufacturing industry show a similar trend. While public investment made a negative contribution to GDP growth in the first quarter of 2000, private consumption is reported to have increased by nearly 5 per cent and added a full percentage point to quarterly GDP growth, with investment and net exports accounting for the rest.

So far the failure of domestic private demand to recover is largely the result of continued adjustment to overinvestment that took place during the boom years of the late 1980s, including elimination of excess capacity and labour. The unemployment rate is now nearing 5 per cent, and real wages have hardly risen as nominal wage declines often exceed the decline in consumer prices. In response to the increased uncertainty over their future income, households have raised their savings rate. According to a Bank of Japan study, "in recent years, income risk is functioning as a factor to increase savings rates, especially for the low- and middle-income households".[4] It is also noted that these are precisely the income groups that have suffered the largest rise in unemployment. Thus, private consumption is unlikely to make an independent contribution to cyclical recovery until the process of restructuring of the Japanese economy is completed. This may still take some time, since surveys suggest that Japanese firms still consider that they have excess capacity and excess labour.

With erratic household spending, rising savings ratios, excess capacity and falling prices, there is little to drive private investment except the need to restructure and the response to recovery in East Asia. Recent figures show that capital investment in industry rose by 3.3 per cent in the first quarter of 2000 on a year-on-year basis, for the first time in nine quarters. At the same time, profits before tax of manufacturing firms rose for the fifth straight quarter, with an increase by more than 40 per cent in the first quarter of 2000, suggesting that a certain amount of restructuring is taking place. Lending by domestic commercial banks also stopped declining in the first quarter, suggesting that government programmes to restructure the banking system are starting to bear fruit.

Japan has been a major beneficiary of the recovery in East Asia thanks mainly to the large presence of Japanese producers in the region. Thus, after falling sharply in 1998 Japanese exports rose rapidly in 1999 despite the appreciation of the yen, with the increase reaching 30 per cent for exports to the Republic of Korea. Capital goods and spare parts accounted for much of this increase as Japanese-owned assembly facilities have boosted imports from Japan to raise production in response to a strong demand for ICT products in the United States, Europe and Japan itself, as well as in the domestic markets of the countries concerned. As in the past, appreciation of the yen has created a more profitable operating environment outside of Japan, but this time Japanese firms have responded by raising production in their existing subsidiaries in East Asia rather than relocating production through new investment in the region. Thus, the situation does not seem to be similar to the previous period of the high yen and the "hollowing out" of Japanese industry. Outward FDI flows from Japan show a decline to Indonesia, Malaysia and Thailand from the already sharply reduced levels of 1998, and only flows to the Republic of Korea have increased.

The expansion in the first quarter of 2000 appears to be more balanced than in 1999 and is evenly spread between domestic private spending and exports. Public spending is no longer the major determinant. Despite the experience of rapid expansion followed by a downturn on several occasions in the past,[5] it can be concluded that the risk of continued recession has passed. However, there remain a number of risks. As a result of public expenditure programmes that have been supporting the economy, fiscal deficits now amount to 10 per cent of GDP and public debt to 105 per cent. A too hasty attempt to reverse public deficits might cut off recovery, as occurred in the past with the restoration of the consumption tax in 1997 or the sudden cessation of spending programmes. The lesson of the United States may be instructive here. In that country the reduction in fiscal deficits was in the context of rapid economic growth which helped to raise productivity trends. In Japan, the prospective 2 per cent growth is insufficient to permit fiscal action to reduce the deficit over and above what is already implicit in the running down of existing public expenditure programmes.

The central bank has been operating a policy of virtual zero intervention rates, while real interest rates are still positive because of the fall in prices. The official position is that the zero rate policy will continue as long as deflationary pressures persist. The policy has had the impact of reducing long-term interest rates to relatively low levels compared with the past. Many long-term securities have been purchased by banks, hoping to profit from the yield differential between short and long rates. Were long-term rates to rise substantially as a result of tightening by the central bank before recovery is fully in place, there would be substantial losses on banks' bond portfolios, which would restrict their ability to provide the domestic financing needed to support the recovery. Recent hints by the central bank that the policy will not be pursued indefinitely may constitute an admonition to financial institutions to make the necessary restructuring now rather than an indication of policy reversal, since recovery has not yet been translated into rising prices and there seems to be virtually no risk of overheating or inflation.

3. European Union

Forecasters have been surprised not only by the continued strong growth of the United States economy in 1999, but also by the failure of Europe to embark on a strong recovery which had been widely expected to allow it to relieve the United States of its role as the main engine of global expansion. Indeed, as anticipated in last year's *TDR*, Europe had difficulty in 1999 in achieving growth in excess of 2 per cent and was unable even to maintain the 1998 rate. Full recovery from the downturn that began in the early 1990s thus still remains to be achieved. Europe now appears not so much to have an asynchronous cyclical relationship with the United States as to have a stable potential growth rate that is increasingly divergent from that of the United States. While on current trends growth is generally expected to reach 3 per cent in 2000, a number of possible developments may lead to a weakening in the second half of the year, including higher interest rates, a partial recovery of the euro, and a slowdown in the United States and East Asia.

While the process of integration continues to produce monetary and financial convergence in "Euroland", growth divergence among the member countries does not seem to be declining. There are significant growth differentials between the larger and the smaller members of European Monetary Union (EMU); in 1999 growth in most major economies, including Germany and Italy, was less than 2 per cent while in the smaller economies, such as Finland, Ireland, Netherlands and Portugal, it was much higher. Monetary tightening, while appropriate for some of the smaller economies showing signs of overheating, makes it more difficult for the larger economies to expand. In the absence of centrally coordinated fiscal measures, there is little prospect for convergence of growth rates.

One of the major reasons for the establishment of EMU was to create a single, unified internal market, with a common currency, that was sufficiently large to be isolated from external shocks, particularly those emanating from the United States, and to free monetary policy from the need to keep intra-European exchange rates stable. Somewhat paradoxically, the successful integration of European financial markets has occurred at the same time as the closer integration of global financial markets, and the introduction of the euro has made the integration of European assets into global portfolios even more rapid. As a result, capital flows to Europe, and hence European interest rates, have become much more responsive to interest rates in the United States. The volatility of United States interest rates has thus started to exert a greater constraint on European monetary policy at a time when the introduction of the euro was expected to give greater policy autonomy.

As has occurred on several occasions in the past, the European recovery is taking place just as the United States expansion is reaching a point that is deemed unsustainable by the country's monetary authorities. Increases in United States interest rates have so far been mirrored by the European Central Bank, despite the fact that inflation in EU continues to be contained around the target rate of 2 per cent and that growth is below potential. Indeed, with unemployment rates still above 9 per cent, several years of growth at above potential could be achieved without running into labour or other supply constraints. Thus monetary tightening appropriate for an economy growing in excess of 6 per cent is being applied in Europe, which is growing less than half as fast.

It has been widely observed that the creation of the single currency turned 11 countries that were individually extremely dependent on external trade into one single currency area, in which external trade and the exchange rate no longer play a major role in determining the level of economic activity, since all intra-European transactions take place as if they were domestic transactions. By the same token, growth in the 11 countries would largely depend on domestic demand, and there was considerable optimism regarding the impact of the introduction of the single currency itself on internal demand and growth. Such expectations are yet to be fulfilled. Indeed, one of the main reasons for the lack of expansion in the larger economies, such as Germany, has been the failure of domestic demand to expand. Ironically, therefore, the failure of domestic demand to expand rapidly has meant that European recovery has become more dependent on external demand. For example, quarterly rates of increase in German net exports to the United States in 1999 were in the range of 10–20 per cent. The EU ran a small surplus with the United States in 1998, with an increase in net exports of $8 billion over the preceding year. In the first three quarters of 1999 its trade surplus continued to grow, more than doubling in the third quarter alone.

The initial estimates of GDP growth in EU for the first quarter of 2000 show an annual expansion of 3.2 per cent relative to the first quarter of 1999. Although household consumption was relatively stagnant, private investment rose by over 2 per cent, in large part due to higher investment in manufacturing associated with increased exports. Whether this first-quarter growth rate can be sustained throughout 2000, to result in an annual growth exceeding 3 per cent, will thus depend on global markets and recovery in consumer spending. Since there is evidence of a slowing in East Asia and the United States, it is unlikely that exports will continue to rise at the rates experienced in 1999. Further, rising European interest rates can be expected to check investment spending. Finally, in addition to falling global demand European exporters may lose competitiveness as a result of a recovery of the euro. Clearly, if there is a substantial slowdown in the United States and a sharp correction in the dollar, European recovery will again be cut off before it has had a chance to work through to higher household incomes and consumption.

The absence of strong consumer spending is not the only difference between Europe and the United States. The high-tech investments associated with the creation of new companies floated on the equity market, and the consequent spinoffs for the financial and services sectors, have yet to appear in Europe. The contribution of information- and computer-related production to growth is estimated at around half a percentage point of GDP in Italy and Germany – only one third of what it is in the United States.[6] As long as European growth remains dependent on external demand rather than consumer spending and technological innovation and restructuring, it is difficult for Europe to replicate the experience of the United States and to replace that country as the engine of global growth.

C. Developing countries

1. Latin America

The economic situation in Latin America deteriorated further in 1999 following a relatively poor performance in the previous year. The region continued to suffer from the impact of the international financial crises for a second consecutive year, as economic downturns deepened in many countries in the wake of the Russian crisis of August 1998. Aggregate output of the region stagnated for the first time since 1990, after growth had fallen to less than 2 per cent in 1998 from 5.3 per cent in 1997 (table 2.2). The outcome, in terms of GDP per capita, was a contraction of 1.3 per cent.

The regional average for 1999 masks not only sharp differences among countries, but also di-

Table 2.2

GROWTH IN DEVELOPING COUNTRIES BY REGION, 1990–1999

(Percentage change over previous year)

Region/country	1990–1995[a]	1996	1997	1998	1999[b]
Latin America	3.6	3.6	5.3	1.9	0.1
of which:					
Argentina	5.8	5.5	8.0	3.9	-2.9
Bolivia	4.1	4.5	4.1	4.6	1.0
Brazil	3.1	2.5	3.5	-0.1	0.8
Chile	8.7	6.9	6.8	3.1	-1.1
Colombia	4.7	2.1	3.4	0.5	-5.2
Ecuador	3.4	2.3	3.9	1.0	-7.3
Mexico	1.4	5.4	6.8	5.0	3.6
Paraguay	3.2	1.1	2.4	-0.6	0.5
Peru	5.5	2.3	8.6	0.1	3.8
Uruguay	3.7	5.0	5.0	4.6	-3.4
Venezuela	3.4	-0.4	6.6	-0.2	-7.2
Africa	1.3	5.2	3.0	3.0	2.7
of which:					
Algeria	0.1	3.8	1.1	5.1	3.4
Cameroon	-1.9	5.0	5.1	5.0	4.4
Côte d'Ivoire	1.9	6.8	6.0	4.5	4.3
Egypt	3.4	4.3	5.0	5.3	6.0
Ghana	4.3	3.5	4.2	4.6	5.5
Kenya	1.6	4.1	2.1	2.1	1.8
Mozambique	3.3	7.1	11.3	12.0	9.7
Nigeria	2.4	6.4	3.1	1.9	1.1
South Africa	0.8	4.2	2.5	0.6	1.2
Uganda	7.0	7.8	4.5	5.4	7.8
Zimbabwe	0.6	8.7	3.7	2.5	0.5
Asia	6.1	6.8	5.9	0.9	5.1
Newly industrializing economies	6.9	6.2	5.8	-2.6	7.5
Hong Kong, China	5.3	4.5	5.0	-5.1	2.9
Republic of Korea	7.4	6.8	5.0	-6.7	10.7
Singapore	8.6	7.5	8.4	0.4	5.4
Taiwan Province of China	6.4	5.7	6.8	4.7	5.5
ASEAN-4	7.0	7.4	3.1	-9.6	2.8
Indonesia	7.1	8.0	4.5	-13.2	0.2
Malaysia	8.7	10.0	7.5	-7.5	5.4
Philippines	2.2	5.8	5.2	-0.5	3.2
Thailand	8.6	5.9	-1.8	-10.4	4.2
ASEAN-4 plus Republic of Korea	7.2	7.1	4.0	-8.2	6.5
South Asia	4.5	6.5	5.1	4.5	6.0
Bangladesh	4.4	5.1	5.3	4.7	4.3
India	4.5	7.1	5.8	4.7	6.8
Nepal	5.2	4.0	1.9	4.0	5.0
Pakistan	4.8	5.0	1.2	3.3	3.1
Sri Lanka	5.4	3.8	6.4	4.7	4.0
West Asia	1.3	4.4	5.5	2.6	0.0
China	12.0	9.6	8.8	7.8	7.1

Source: UNCTAD secretariat calculations, based on data in 1995 dollars.
   a Annual average.
   b Estimated.

verse developments within economies in the course of the year. Close links to the United States economy through *maquila* and other industrial exports and tourism gave Mexico the best performance amongst the large economies, but only with a modest growth of 3.6 per cent. The economies of Central America and the Caribbean also benefited from the continued United States expansion, and growth was as high as 6–7 per cent in some of the smaller economies (e.g. Costa Rica, Dominican Republic and Nicaragua).

By contrast, most South American countries experienced deep recessions, with output falling by more than 5 per cent in Colombia, Ecuador, and Venezuela. Even Chile registered negative growth, for the first time in 15 years. The sharp turnaround in oil prices was a key factor in limiting the impact on output of natural disasters in Venezuela, while in Ecuador there was political turmoil and continued financial instability. In Colombia, the economic situation was aggravated by internal armed conflict, while El Salvador and Honduras have yet to recover fully from the devastation caused by hurricanes in 1998.

Adjustment policies similar to those that had been employed after the financial crisis in East Asia were initially adopted in response to the adverse spillovers from financial crises, including high interest rates and fiscal tightening to defend exchange-rate arrangements and to maintain market confidence. As in East Asia, these policies led to a slowdown in economic activity, accentuating or initiating recessions. As described in chapter III, some countries (Brazil, Chile and Colombia) were forced to abandon their currency bands and float their currencies in the course of 1999, but the subsequent depreciations have not led to a rapid acceleration of inflation: for the third year in a row inflation was around 10 per cent for the region, the lowest level in half a century.

Notwithstanding the poor performance of the region in 1999, the overall output growth turned out to be better than initially expected, mainly because of a rapid turnaround in economic activity in Brazil, which accounts for some 40 per cent of the region's output. The difference in performance between Brazil and Argentina provides a useful contrast for comparing alternative policy approaches. Until the beginning of 1999 policies in both countries were designed to defend exchange-rate regimes through high interest rates and fiscal restraint. High interest rates had caused structural imbalances as the interest cost of outstanding government debt more than offset primary budget surpluses and the increased servicing costs of foreign debt offset improvements in export performance. As a result, both countries experienced a progressive loss of international investor confidence and severe pressures on their external payments positions.

As discussed in last year's *TDR*, since most foreign investors and Brazilian banks had been expecting the exchange-rate adjustment, capital outflows after the suspension of the peg were not substantial. Continued privatization sales to foreigners, as well as the return of optimism due to increased competitiveness and relaxation of policies, produced a recovery of FDI inflows. The currency stabilized and interest rates were steadily reduced, providing a sharp reduction in the fiscal deficit and improvement in external debt servicing. Belying widespread forecasts of a contraction of some 4 per cent in 1999, the economy managed to grow by about 1 per cent. Annual growth in the first quarter of 2000 was above 3 per cent, with manufacturing output registering an increase of nearly 8 per cent over the same quarter a year earlier. The trade balance remained in deficit; export earnings fell by 7.5 per cent, while imports contracted by almost 15 per cent.

In contrast to Brazil, which has had a better than anticipated growth performance after the collapse of the currency, Argentina's growth has been below expectations after the successful defence of its dollar peg. In addition to the sharp reduction in exports to Brazil as a result of the currency adjustment, Argentina was adversely affected by high real interest rates needed to support the exchange rate, and by low grain prices. Furthermore, falling domestic prices reduced government revenues, requiring expenditure cuts and wage reductions in the public sector to meet fiscal targets agreed with IMF. Average wages per worker in manufacturing were down almost 4 per cent in the fourth quarter of 1999 from a year earlier, and the fall in consumer prices continued, down 1 per cent in May 2000 from a year earlier. Thus Argentina is facing a full-scale price deflation, and is attempting to reduce costs and expenditures in step; creating further downside risks. While conditions somewhat stabilized in the fourth quarter of 1999, expectations of growth, ranging from 2.6 per cent to 4.0 per cent (see table 2.4 below) in 2000 may not be realized, as the only net contributor to growth is net exports. The economy would be adversely affected by a continued increase in United States interest rates or continued strength in the dollar, requiring another downward adjustment of wages and prices, which is the normal mechanism of adjustment for countries operating a currency-board regime.

For Latin America as a whole, the trade deficit improved significantly in 1999 mainly as a result of a contraction of imports, resulting in a sharp reduction in the current-account deficit from $87.5 billion (4.5 per cent of GDP) in 1998 to $56.5 billion (3.2 per cent). Falling capital inflows (described in chapter III) and rising profit remittances combined to produce a sharp contraction in the net transfer of resources. Only a few countries, notably those in Central America, attracted more capital. Because of the decline in total inflows, many countries had to resort to the use of international reserves and compensatory borrowing. Brazil, by contrast, repaid some of the official debt incurred during the currency crisis. Mexico, on the other hand, has been accumulating excess reserves as a hedge against possible financial turmoil in the aftermath of its July general election.

For 2000, the prospects for Latin America depend very much on the evolution of the external economic environment and the scope to use monetary and fiscal policy to support domestic demand. If global output and world trade continue to improve, the United States market remains buoyant and interest rates are kept stable, growth for the region as a whole may reach 4 per cent. Although the pickup in growth will be general, it will also be uneven in view of various country-specific factors. Recovery in countries such as Colombia, Ecuador, Guatemala, Peru and Venezuela is likely to be hindered by the problems in their fragile financial sectors.

2. Asia

In developing Asia as a whole, excluding China, there was a sharp upturn in 1999, with growth reaching some 4.4 per cent, compared to a slight contraction in the previous year. However, the strength of economic activity and the timing of recovery varied considerably among countries. While growth came to a halt in West Asia, it accelerated somewhat in South Asia. By contrast, in East Asia, in both the newly industrializing economies (NIEs) and ASEAN-4, there was a strong recovery from the deep recession of 1998.

Economic activity in *West Asia* stagnated in 1999 despite a strong recovery in oil prices. While performance improved somewhat in a number of oil-importing countries, such as Israel and Jordan, growth remained weak in Saudi Arabia and Kuwait as a result of lower oil output. There was a sharp contraction in Turkey due to the August earthquake and spillovers from the financial crisis in the Russian Federation.

Prospects of the region continue to be dominated by developments in the oil market and progress in the Middle East peace process. Inasmuch as the economic contraction in Turkey appears to have bottomed out, aggregate output of West Asia is expected to pick up markedly in 2000 as the effects of the sharp rise in oil prices and revenues filter through to higher consumption and a recovery of investment in oil-exporting countries. In the countries of the Gulf Cooperation Council,[7] unemployment continues to be high. As oil continues to account in most countries of the region for about 40 per cent of GDP and over 80 per cent of government receipts, they remain highly vulnerable to fluctuations in oil prices. The oil-importing countries are also affected, through the impact on the level of grants and workers' remittances. The lack of notable progress in the Middle East peace process, as well as the economic sanctions on Iraq, continues to discourage intraregional trade, investment and tourism, thereby impeding a strong and sustained recovery.

The economic performance of the countries of *South Asia* in 1999 was mixed. The acceleration in GDP growth from 4.5 per cent in 1998 to 6.0 per cent for the subregion is primarily a reflection of the strength of the Indian economy, whereas there was a mild slowdown in Bangladesh and Pakistan (table 2.2). The diversity of performance is attributable to differences in various factors, including climatic and political conditions as well as domestic policy and structural problems. Overall, external conditions were relatively favourable, and for both India and Pakistan the negative effects of the economic sanctions following nuclear tests were no longer in evidence. In Pakistan, the economic sanctions were partially waived in January 1999 and international financial institutions subsequently resumed their assistance.

The acceleration in growth in India is accounted for by industry and services, where faster growth more than offset the sharp slowdown in agricultural growth to less than 1 per cent, from 7.2 per cent in the previous year, as a result of erratic monsoon in some areas and serious damage caused by a cyclone that struck the Orissa coast in October 1999. In Pakistan, continued political instability, acute balance-of-payments problems and macroeconomic imbalance resulted in a moderate slowdown in 1999. Growth also slowed in Bangladesh, where manufacturing was seriously hampered by floods during the first half of 1999 and by political instability, as well as in Sri Lanka, due to declining industrial output. For most countries in the subregion, notably India and Sri Lanka, fiscal imbalances continue to be a cause for concern. Nevertheless, growth momentum is expected to continue in 2000, with modest improvements in some countries.

The *East Asian* economies that were in severe recession in 1998 as a result of the financial crisis made a spectacular recovery in 1999. Signs of a revival became evident in the first half of the year and the momentum has continued into 2000. As discussed in greater detail in chapter IV, the recovery was initiated by the reversal of contractionary monetary and fiscal policies, which was eventually reinforced by a recovery in exports that brought to an end the process of severe import compression and destocking. The high degree of regional integration that had been a major factor responsible for contagion and poor export performance worked to bring about a significant improvement in exports in 1999.[8] Exports were also helped by currency depreciations as well as the buoyancy of the United States market. Of particular importance to Malaysia, the Philippines, Singapore, Taiwan Province of China and Thailand was a surge in worldwide demand for electronics associated with the rapid and sustained expansion of the IT sector in developed countries, as well as the response to the Y2K computer bug risk noted in the introduction to this chapter.

The combination of expansionary policies and rising exports helped to increase capacity utilization rates, stabilized unemployment and brought a recovery to domestic consumption that was reflected in higher imports towards the end of the period. As described in chapter III, there was a rise in private capital inflows into the region, primarily in the form of FDI that was driven in part by foreign acquisition of companies in financial distress.

Aggregate GDP of the four NIEs rebounded strongly in 1999, growing by 7.5 per cent, compared to a contraction in the previous year (table 2.2). However, performance varied significantly. After a sharp decline in 1998, growth in the Republic of Korea exceeded 10 per cent, the highest rate since 1988. The recovery in Hong Kong (China) was much less spectacular. The turnaround, which also brought recovery in local asset markets, started in the second quarter of 1999, after six consecutive quarters of decline, and was reinforced by improved conditions in neighbouring economies. Growth in Singapore was stronger, after virtual stagnation in 1998, mainly due to the strong external demand for ICT-related products, but the non-electronic segment of manufacturing also performed well.

In contrast to most other economies in the region, Taiwan Province of China suffered relatively little from the East Asian financial turmoil, thanks to its pre-emptive devaluation and large foreign exchange reserves. Nevertheless, output growth slowed to a 15-year low of 4.7 per cent in 1998. There was a modest pickup in 1999, but productive capacity and physical infrastructure suffered considerably from the earthquake in September 1999.[9] Reconstruction of damaged structures may provide a major stimulus to economic activity.

The ASEAN-4 economies all grew in 1999 after output contractions in 1998, which ranged from less than 1 per cent in the Philippines to as much as 13 per cent in Indonesia. The Philippines managed to avoid a deep recession thanks to its strong export performance arising from closer trade ties with the United States market. After an initially tenuous start in early 1999, recovery in the subregion became more rapid and broad-based than anticipated (table 2.2).

Growth in developing Asia in 2000 can be expected to be more balanced among countries than in 1999, with the rate slowing to 7–8 per cent in the Republic of Korea, while recovery in ASEAN-4 is expected to gather momentum: Malaysian growth, which reached double-digit figures in the first months of 2000, will have to be moderated to prevent a return to the labour shortage conditions experienced before the crisis. There are considerable downside risks for Indonesia; Hong Kong (China) will be affected by the impending accession of China to WTO, but the immediate effects are uncertain.

The economy of *China* continued to perform relatively well in 1999, with growth exceeding 7 per cent, thanks in part to the recovery of other economies in East Asia and in part also to various fiscal packages. This relatively rapid growth was nonetheless low by Chinese standards; it was the slowest rate in the past decade, representing the seventh successive decline since the peak of 14.2 per cent in 1992. Moreover, the economy is characterized by price deflation, over-production and excess capacity. The continued fall in prices since mid-1997, together with the appreciation of other currencies in the region, has helped to reverse the real appreciation of the yuan and stimulate exports, which have also benefited from export tax rebates.

Faced with the challenge to counter near-term deflationary forces generated by structural reforms, the Chinese Government has continued since mid-1998 to ease monetary and fiscal policy, and implemented a series of measures, such as large infrastructure spending and cuts in interest rates, to boost domestic demand. However, the impact on consumer spending and investment other than that undertaken by the Central Government has been minimal. Consumer confidence has remained low, mainly because of job and income insecurity arising from growing unemployment and restructuring of State-owned enterprises (SOEs). The annualized rate of expansion of fixed investment fell in 1999 from 15 per cent in May to negative numbers in September, as compared to increases of over 40 per cent per annum during 1992–1995.

Although the Chinese economy was not subject to direct contagion from the Asian crisis, the collapse of the region's capital markets had an adverse impact on capital inflows. The total FDI inflow into China stagnated in 1998 and declined by 11 per cent in 1999. Efforts made since early 1998 to restructure or privatize SOEs ran into difficulty as the urban unemployment rate climbed to politically and socially unacceptable levels (7–8 per cent), and the authorities were obliged to allow social stability to take priority over reform. However, the reform of SOEs continues to be a major objective of economic policy.

In the search for new sources of economic growth, greater importance is being attached to opportunities in the country's less developed interior, a shift which was already visible in the five-year plan for 1991–1995. In January 2000,

the State Council set up a high-level inter-ministerial Western Development Committee, charged with the task of mapping out long-term strategies to guide the development of China's western provinces over the next 15 years. The development of the western region also constituted an important item on the agenda of the 9th National People's Congress in March 2000, and 70 per cent of total fixed investment in the budget for 2000 has been earmarked for developing the infrastructure of the western regions.

Apart from providing an immediate boost to economic growth, focus on the new development frontier provides a means for the Chinese authorities to address the increasingly glaring income disparities between the coastal areas and the interior. Per capita GDP on the coast is more than double that of any province in the interior, which contains two thirds of China's population. Furthermore, successful economic development of the western regions over the longer run will help to reduce poverty and ethnic tensions, as well as protect the environment and reduce population pressure on the coast. The western region, however, is not a homogenous entity. Some parts are more developed than others because of richer natural resources or investment in defence-related heavy industry. Land-locked provinces such as Gansu and Ningxia are likely to remain trapped in poverty for some time.

Although the fall in prices appears to be bottoming out, the government is not likely to reverse its expansionary fiscal policy. Fiscal stimulus and rising exports should keep GDP growth within the 7–8 per cent range in 2000. China's impending membership of WTO is expected to provide a timely boost to economic growth by helping to expand exports and attract new FDI, but it may also lead to considerable adjustment costs, at least in the short term. The precise effect of membership is difficult to predict and depends, *inter alia*, on how the agreements with various parties are interpreted and implemented.

3. Africa

Output growth in Africa in 1999 was slightly lower than the 3.0 per cent attained in the previous two years, barely keeping pace with population growth (table 2.2). The poor economic performance of the region in the past three years, following relatively strong growth in 1996, suggests that domestic and external conditions are nowhere close to what is needed to produce the much hoped-for take-off into rapid and sustained growth, particularly in sub-Saharan Africa.

Average growth rates in both East and North Africa in 1999 were significantly higher than in other subregions. Relative to 1998 growth was lower in Central, North and West Africa, but higher in East and Southern Africa.[10] Continuing armed conflict and civil unrest have severely undermined economic performance in a number of countries, notably in the Great Lakes region of Central Africa, and, as in the Ethiopia-Eritrea border conflict, contributed to poor performance in neighbouring countries. Similarly, differing weather conditions have played an important role in the variation of economic performance among subregions. Vulnerability to such conditions is once more shown by the effects of recent floods in Southern Africa in the aftermath of two tropical storms in February 2000, which hit a number of countries, including Botswana, Madagascar, Mozambique, Namibia, Zambia and Zimbabwe, and caused significant loss of lives, displacement of population and extensive damage to crops and infrastructure.

Economic performance in Central Africa, which accounts for about 6 per cent of the continent's GDP, is highly dependent on world prices of oil and other primary commodities, notably coffee, cocoa, timber and copper. Growth in both Cameroon and Rwanda was lower in 1999 than in 1998 but still considerably higher than the overall regional average. Depressed coffee prices offset the benefits of higher oil prices for Cameroon, and of stronger performance of agriculture and services, due largely to FDI from South Africa and aid inflows, in Rwanda. The prices of these commodities will continue to have an significant influence on growth in 2000.

In East Africa, which accounts for about 7 per cent of the continent's output, some countries have been adversely affected by armed conflicts. Performance in Kenya has been disappointing in recent years due to deteriorating infrastructure, increased labour unrest, and a loss of investor confidence. By contrast, growth accelerated sharply in Uganda, due in part to official debt relief, increased FDI, and recovery in agriculture. Despite uncertainties associated with its dependence on rain-fed agriculture, East Africa is

expected to maintain a moderate pace of growth in the years ahead.

Economic growth in North Africa, which accounts for 39 per cent of the continent's overall output, was adversely affected by civil war and political instability in the 1990s, but prospects have improved in recent years. Growth increased moderately in Egypt in 1999 due largely to a strong performance of agriculture (wheat production more than doubled) and higher oil prices, but fell sharply in Algeria as unfavourable weather reduced farm output. This was also the case in Morocco and Tunisia. Weather conditions, together with oil prices, will continue to be determining factors in these countries.

The poor performance of Southern Africa in recent years is a reflection of the situation in South Africa, which accounts for 85 per cent of the output of the subregion. While its economy had been adversely affected by the financial contagion from the Asian crisis and weak commodity prices, especially of gold, its leading export, the decline in economic activity appears to have bottomed out in 1999. Growth in Mozambique, one of the fastest-growing economies in the world, slowed in 1999, but in spite of the devastating flood it is likely to reach 5 per cent this year.

Armed conflicts and political instability have also affected several countries in West Africa, which accounts for 13 per cent of Africa's output. The CFA economies have continued to perform well since the large devaluation of the CFA franc in 1994. The decline of the euro against the dollar has also improved their competitiveness at a time when the prices of some of their main exports, especially cocoa, coffee, cotton, gold and some metals, were depressed. The upturn in CFA economies in 1999 was more than offset by the slowdown in other countries of West Africa, due mainly to lower prices for some of their leading exports, especially cocoa, timber and natural rubber. Growth in Nigeria, by far the largest economy in the subregion and highly dependent on oil (which accounts for over 96 per cent of export earnings and 80 per cent of government revenues), has continued to fall after peaking in 1996. The decline was due to the reduced oil output following the lowering of OPEC quotas and civil unrest in oil-producing regions, although the adverse effects were mitigated to some extent by higher prices and faster growth in the non-oil sector.

An important factor in the variation of economic performance among African countries is disparate changes in commodity prices, since different countries' exports are concentrated on different commodities.[11] The strengthening of prices of industrial commodities such as oil and copper, compared to continued weak prices of beverages, especially a sharp downturn in cocoa and coffee prices, played an important role in the relative economic performance of these countries. In particular, while higher oil prices have increased export earnings and government revenue in oil-exporting countries, their adverse impact on the balance of payments and inflation has been acute for oil-importing countries.

Short-term growth prospects depend on the prices of oil and non-oil commodities; the CFA countries will also be affected by the movement of the euro against the dollar. Growth may rise moderately in 2000 if oil prices remain at relatively high levels and other commodity prices strengthen. Even so, much of the growth is likely to be concentrated in North Africa. Growth may also accelerate in South Africa following the sluggish performance of 1998 and early 1999.

For most sub-Saharan African economies, growth in the longer term remains constrained by low savings and investment and foreign-exchange gaps. In this connection official capital inflows can play a crucial role in setting off a faster and sustained growth and eventually reducing the dependence of the region on aid. According to estimates by the UNCTAD secretariat, if growth in sub-Saharan Africa could be raised to some 6 per cent per annum and sustained at that rate for at least a decade, through a large injection of aid accompanied by appropriate domestic policies, the need for official financing would gradually diminish as alternative sources of financing came forward. First, rapidly rising income would allow domestic savings to be raised faster than output, thereby closing the savings gap. Secondly, sustaining growth would attract private capital, as a substitute for official financing.[12]

Clearly, debt relief can play a role in this process. In this respect, some progress has been made over the past year in the context of the Initiative for the Heavily Indebted Poor Countries (HIPC), including: modifying the framework so as to lower debt sustainability targets, thereby enlarging the number of countries eligible for assistance; the provision of enhanced interim relief once countries are declared eligible; and the possibility to complete the HIPC process more rapidly for countries implementing strong reform and poverty reduction programmes. The total number of HIPCs expected to become eligible under the enhanced initiative has risen from 29 to 36, of which 30 are in sub-Saharan Africa. However, even if the enhanced HIPC initiative is fully and rapidly implemented, the scale of its impact will be limited. Many African countries are unable to meet their external debt-servicing obligations, and for them debt relief will simply formally acknowledge a situation that already exists and stop the cumulation of arrears which are unlikely ever to be paid.

D. Transition economies[13]

GDP in the transition economies as a whole increased by 2.4 per cent in 1999, the highest rate in the past decade. The overall figure, however, masks an unusual degree of volatility during the year, as well as considerable variations among countries. Output grew unexpectedly by some 3 per cent in the Commonwealth of Independent States (CIS) as a whole, compared to 1.4 per cent for Eastern Europe, whereas the Baltic States plunged into sharp recession (table 2.3).

Economic growth slowed sharply in virtually all the transition economies at the beginning of 1999 largely as a consequence of the effects of the East Asian and Russian financial crises, aggravated in some cases by the conflict in Kosovo

Table 2.3

TRANSITION ECONOMIES: SELECTED ECONOMIC INDICATORS, 1997–1999

	GDP			Consumer prices			Current-account balance		
	Change over previous year[a]								
	(Percentage)						(Percentage of GDP)		
Region/country	1997	1998	1999	1997	1998	1999	1997	1998	1999[b]
Eastern Europe	2.1	1.8	1.4	..	..	..	-4.3	-4.6	-5.5
of which:									
Bulgaria	-7.0	3.5	2.6	578.7	0.9	6.2	4.2	-0.5	-5.5
Croatia	6.8	2.5	-0.3	4.0	5.6	4.6	-11.5	-7.1	-7.2
Czech Republic	-1.0	-2.2	-0.2	9.9	6.7	2.5	-6.1	-2.4	-2.0
Hungary	4.6	4.9	4.5	18.4	10.4	11.3	-2.1	-4.9	-4.3
Poland	6.9	4.8	4.1	13.2	8.5	9.9	-3.0	-4.4	-7.5
Romania	-6.1	-5.4	-3.2	151.7	40.7	54.9	-6.1	-7.2	-3.8
Slovakia	6.5	4.4	1.9	6.5	5.5	14.4	-10.0	-10.1	-5.7
Slovenia	4.6	3.9	4.9	8.8	6.6	8.1	0.2	–	-3.0
Baltic States	8.4	4.5	-1.7	..	..	..	-9.5	-11.1	-9.6
Estonia	10.6	4.0	-1.4	12.3	6.8	3.9	-12.2	-9.2	-4.9
Latvia	8.6	3.9	0.1	7.0	2.8	3.3	-6.1	-11.1	-12.1
Lithuania	7.3	5.1	-3.0	8.5	2.4	0.3	-10.2	-12.1	-10.3
CIS	1.1	-3.0	2.9	..	..	..	-0.4	-1.4	6.7
of which:									
Belarus	11.4	8.4	3.4	63.4	181.6	251.3	-5.9	-7.5	-0.4
Russian Federation	0.9	-4.9	3.2	11.0	84.5	36.7	0.9	0.7	11.2
Ukraine	-3.0	-1.7	-0.4	10.1	20.0	19.2	-2.7	-3.1	3.3

Source: ECE, *Economic Survey of Europe 2000,* no. 1. United Nations publication, sales no. E.00.II.E.12, New York and Geneva, 2000, tables 3.1.1 and 3.1.2.

a For consumer prices change from December to December.

b Full year for Eastern Europe and Baltic States; January–September for CIS. Current-account balances for the Baltic States are based on extrapolations of January–September trends.

and a slowdown in import demand in Western Europe. The Russian crisis had severe consequences particularly for the Baltic economies, where it resulted in large cuts in exports to the Russian Federation and a severe deterioration in output and employment. However, the unwinding of various factors in the second half of 1999 led to a marked improvement in Central Europe and a more moderate one in the Baltic States. The recovery in exports to EU was important, especially for Central Europe, but for the Baltic countries it was not sufficient to offset the loss in the CIS markets. At more than 4 per cent, growth in Hungary, Poland and Slovenia was considerably faster than the 2.4 per cent average for the transition

economies, thanks in large part to strong domestic demand. The biggest surprise in 1999 was the recovery in the Russian Federation, where GDP rose by over 3 per cent, in contrast to an expected fall of 2.5 per cent, thanks to the sharp rise in oil prices and the devaluation of the rouble.

Discernible also in 1999 in the transition economies was increased inflation. The process of steady disinflation which had been under way for several years was interrupted; in most economies price increases were larger than in 1998, especially in the countries members of CIS, which were affected by the devaluation of the rouble. Primarily responsible for higher inflation in many other economies was the sharp increase in the world price of crude oil, together with the appreciation of the dollar.

Relatively weak foreign demand was a major factor in the poor trade performance of many economies in 1999. For the transition economies as a whole, exports fell in both volume and value, but the decline in imports was even steeper (see table 3.1 below). In Eastern Europe, the value of total trade (imports plus exports) fell for the first time since 1991. The contraction in trade was also evident in most of the CIS countries, and was particularly large in the Baltic States.

Deep cuts in imports reflected the tightened balance-of-payments constraint in view of a reduction in capital inflows. Several countries encountered difficulties in obtaining international finance. The net inflow into Eastern Europe and the Baltic States fell below the level of 1998, and there was a large increase in capital outflow from the Russian Federation. The tighter balance-of-payment constraints forced a reduction in domestic demand and imports in a number of economies, notably those of CIS countries (other than the Russian Federation). Current-account balances generally improved, with the exception of Bulgaria and Poland.

As a consequence of the Kosovo conflict, the attention of the international community has been directed to measures needed for the economic regeneration of a specific group of seven South-East European economies,[14] with a view also to strengthening the prospects for both peace and political stability in the area. These are countries which have lagged far behind in the process of transition and have been greatly affected by the Kosovo conflict and its aftermath. Despite modest growth in Bulgaria and The former Yugoslav Republic of Macedonia, output for the group as a whole contracted by nearly 3 per cent in 1999.

The economic problems of South-East Europe are for the most part essentially those of underde-velopment, despite the fact that on a number of indicators, such as education, they are closer to Western Europe than the traditional group of developing countries. In some of them (Albania, Bulgaria, Romania) the legacy of the command system remains much stronger than elsewhere. The macroeconomic situation in most of these economies is still quite fragile. While inflation has been successfully reduced, current-account deficits have been large and persistent, resulting in a rapid accumulation of foreign debt. At 17 per cent, unemployment is much higher than in Central Europe. Domestic investment remains weak and foreign investment is not attracted to the region in any significant amount.

Given the sheer scale of the problems facing the governments of these seven countries, the probability of crises continues to be high, particularly in the absence of sustained and targeted assistance from abroad. International efforts are now extensive, but it is becoming increasingly clear that they suffer from many of the same shortcomings that have beset the programmes of assistance to most other transition economies since 1989, including a large gap between commitments and actual disbursement of aid and poor coordination among the 29 countries and international organizations under the Stability Pact.

For 2000, prospects for the transition economies in general have improved considerably since the beginning of the year. Both domestic conditions and the external environment are more favourable. Growth is expected to average around 3 per cent, ranging from some 4 per cent in Eastern Europe to 3 per cent in the Baltic States and 2 per cent or more in the CIS countries (depending on the developments in the Russian Federation). Reflecting a rebound from a very low base, governments in a number of South-East European transition economies are expecting relatively high growth rates in 2000. The current recovery in the Russian Federation is fragile, but the official forecast of growth for 2000 has now been raised from around 2.0 per cent to more than 4.0 per cent.

E. Prospects and forecasts

While the prospects for the global economy have become increasingly more optimistic since the end of 1999, the risk that global imbalances may create another financial disruption has also strengthened. The better-than-expected performance in 1999, in particular in the United States, East Asia and Brazil, has led to an upward revision of short-term forecasts of growth for all major economic regions. This tendency has been reinforced by the fact that the global economy has continued to gather strength as the expansion of demand and output has become more widespread. However, perceptions of such developments vary considerable among various international organizations and other institutions. As can be seen from table 2.4, the forecast of world output growth in 2000 ranges from 3.5 per cent to 4.3 per cent, compared to an estimated only 2.7 per cent achieved in 1999 (table 2.1). There are also significant differences in growth rates forecast for different regions. For example, there is much uncertainty associated with the widely expected slowdown of the United States economy and the recovery in Japan and Europe, while in the developing world there are questions concerning the sustainability of the rapid expansion in the Republic of Korea and the likelihood of recovery in Argentina.

There are already some clear signals that suggest that the United States economy is starting to slow from its rapid pace of growth at the turn of the year, while the vigour of economic activity in Europe appears to be broadening but without great momentum. This has led to some downward revision of optimistic forecasts for these economies. Recovery in most developing economies in East Asia has been stronger than expected, but there are signs of deceleration. The slowdown in China appears to have bottomed out, but the Chinese authorities still consider stimulus necessary. While recovery in Latin America is under way, the situation in Argentina remains fragile, the financial crisis in Ecuador is unresolved, and the sustainability of recovery in Brazil is crucially dependent on conditions in world markets.

Thus, despite the sharply improved performance of the world economy in 1999 and early 2000, there is much uncertainty concerning the short-term outlook and many challenges remain. For a variety of reasons, the recent steep rise in the price of oil has not had an impact comparable to that of the oil shocks of the 1970s, and is unlikely to have a comparable impact unless there are exceedingly steep increases to follow. At least for the time being, global deflation has replaced inflation as a source of concern, and the shift in monetary policy in most major countries will act as a further brake on continued growth. Exchange-rate and financial instability are always potential threats in the presence of large global imbalances. A sharp appreciation of the yen or lack of progress in structural reforms, for example, could jeopardize the nascent recovery in Japan. The recovery in emerging markets may be adversely affected by rising international interest rates if the United States economy remains excessively strong, or by reduced financial flows in the event of a dollar collapse or a global liquidity crisis. Most forecasts of continued global expansion are based on the "Goldilocks" scenario in which the United States economy is neither too hot nor too cold, allowing Europe and Japan to grow and providing support for continued recovery in Latin America and Asia. In assessing the forecasts for accelerated global growth it is as well to remember that Goldilocks is a fairy tale.

Table 2.4

FORECASTS OF GDP GROWTH IN 2000 BY REGION AND FOR SELECTED COUNTRIES BY VARIOUS INSTITUTIONS

(Percentage change over 1999[a])

	IMF	World Bank	OECD	UN/LINK	JP Morgan
World	4.2	3.5	4.3	3.5	4.1
Industrial countries	3.4	3.2[b]	4.0[b]	3.0	3.7[b]
United States	4.4	3.8	4.9	4.1	4.9
Japan	0.9	1.2	1.7	0.9	1.6
European Union	3.2	.	3.4	3.1	3.8[c]
Germany	2.8	.	2.9	2.5	3.5
France	3.5	.	3.7	3.6	4.0
Italy	2.7	.	2.9	2.6	3.5
United Kingdom	3.0	.	2.9	3.3	3.4
Transition economies	2.6	2.5	.	3.0	5.4[d]
Russian Federation	1.5	.	4.0	2.5	6.5
Developing countries	5.4	5.0	.	5.2	.
Africa	4.4	.	.	4.4	.
Asia	6.2	6.4	.	6.2[e]	6.6[f]
Newly industrializing economies	6.6	5.5	.	.	.
Hong Kong, China	6.0	.	5.2	4.9	6.5
Republic of Korea	7.0	.	8.5	8.2	8.0
Singapore	5.9	.	.	6.7	5.0
Taiwan Province of China	6.2	.	.	6.4	7.0
ASEAN-4	4.0	.	.	.	5.1[g]
Indonesia	3.0	.	3.0	4.3	4.0
Malaysia	6.0	.	6.2	7.2	6.5
Philippines	4.5	.	3.5	4.1	4.5
Thailand	4.5	.	5.5	4.8	6.0
ASEAN-4 plus Republic of Korea	.	5.7	.	.	.
South Asia	.	5.9	.	.	.
China	7.0	.	7.7	7.5	7.0
Latin America	4.0	3.6	.	3.7	4.3
Argentina	3.4	.	2.6	2.8	4.0
Brazil	4.0	.	3.2	3.6	3.7
Mexico	4.5	.	4.8	4.8	5.5

Source: IMF, *World Economic Outlook*, April 2000; World Bank, *Global Development Finance*, April 2000; OECD, *OECD Economic Outlook*, June 2000; UN/LINK, Pre-LINK meeting forecast (April 2000); and JP Morgan, *World Financial Markets*, New York, 14 April 2000.

a Based on weights in terms of purchasing power parity for IMF, World Bank and OECD, and in terms of market exchange rates for LINK and JP Morgan.
b Including also Mexico and the Republic of Korea.
c The 11 EMU countries.
d Bulgaria, Czech Republic, Greece, Hungary, Poland, Russian Federation and Turkey.
e South and East Asia.
f China, Hong Kong (China), India, Indonesia, Malaysia, Philippines, Republic of Korea, Singapore, Taiwan Province of China and Thailand.
g Including also Singapore.   ■

Notes

1 Figures given by individual companies and national estimates are not comparable, since spending on hardware replacement, for example, is not always included. Estimates higher than the $600 billion given by the Gartner Group include $675 by Software Productivity Research and $1,200 billion by Cap Gemini.

2 See *TDR 1998*, Part One, annex to chap. III.

3 Fallows J, Week in review, *New York Times*, 13 February 2000: 3.

4 Shinobu Nakagawa, Why has Japan's household savings rate remained high even during the 1990s?, *Bank of Japan Monthly Bulletin*, April 1999: ii.

5 See the discussion in *TDR 1999* that expressed scepticism of the sustainability of the expansion in 1999.

6 See Crédit Suisse First Boston, The best is not yet to come, *Euro-11 Weekly*, 19 May 2000.

7 Bahrain, Kuwait, Oman, Qatar, Saudi Arabia and United Arab Emirates.

8 For an analysis of this regional interdependence see *TDR 1996*, Part Two, chaps. I and II; and *TDR 1993*, Part Two, chap. IV and annex 3.

9 For example, production losses due to the interruption of power supply to microchip manufacturers at the high-tech industrial park in Hsin-Chu City were estimated to be $320 million. See *Asian Development Outlook 2000*, Asian Development Bank, Manila, 2000: 56.

10 The subregions distinguished in this subsection are as defined by the African Development Bank: (1) Central Africa (Burundi, Cameroon, Central African Republic (CAR), Chad, Congo, Democratic Republic of Congo, Equatorial Guinea, Gabon, Rwanda and Sao Tome and Principe); (2) East Africa (Comoros, Djibouti, Eritrea, Ethiopia, Kenya, Madagascar, Mauritius, Seychelles, Somalia, Uganda and United Republic of Tanzania); (3) North Africa (Algeria, Egypt, Libyan Arab Jamahiriya, Mauritania, Morocco, Sudan and Tunisia); (4) Southern Africa (Angola, Botswana, Lesotho, Malawi, Mozambique, Namibia, South Africa, Swaziland, Zambia and Zimbabwe); and (5) West Africa (CFA countries: Benin, Burkina Faso, Côte d'Ivoire, Guinea-Bissau, Mali, Niger, Senegal and Togo; non-CFA countries: Cape Verde, Ghana, Guinea, Gambia, Nigeria, Liberia and Sierra Leone).

11 Crude oil accounts for more than 95 per cent of total export earnings in Angola, Equatorial Guinea, Gabon and Nigeria, and is also important for Cameroon, Congo and Côte d'Ivoire. South Africa is the world's largest gold producer, but gold is also an important export item for Ghana, Guinea, Mali, Zimbabwe, and (increasingly) the United Republic of Tanzania. Côte d'Ivoire is the world's largest producer of cocoa, which is also important for Ghana. Whereas cocoa is the dominant export crop in West Africa, tea dominates commodity exports for many East and Southern African countries. Next to Kenya, leading African tea exporters include Malawi, Rwanda, Uganda, United Republic of Tanzania and Zimbabwe. Coffee is important in both East and West Africa. Côte d'Ivoire, Ethiopia and Uganda are the region's three largest coffee producers, but Burundi, Cameroon, the Democratic Republic of Congo, Kenya, Madagascar, Rwanda, Togo and the United Republic of Tanzania are also significant exporters.

12 *Capital Flows and Growth in Africa* (UNCTAD/GDS/MDPB/7), New York and Geneva, 2000.

13 This subsection draws on Economic Commission for Europe, *Economic Survey of Europe 2000*, no. 1, United Nations publication, sales no. E.00.II.E.12, New York and Geneva, 2000.

14 Albania, Bosnia and Herzegovina, Bulgaria, Croatia, Romania, The former Yugoslav Republic of Macedonia, and Yugoslavia.

Chapter III

INTERNATIONAL MARKETS

A. Recent developments in international trade

The deep recession and rapid recovery in emerging markets, together with the diverse movements of commodity prices, including oil, have given rise to sharp swings in international trade flows over the past few years as well as to considerable shifts in the commodity terms of trade. The widespread decline in economic activity during 1997–1998 was accompanied by a sharp slowdown in the growth of world trade volumes and, because of falling prices, an absolute decline in the value of world trade. The decline in trade in 1998 was discernible in varying degrees in all developing regions and in the transition economies, but it was especially sharp for African exports and Asian imports.

The revival in world trade in 1999 in the wake of the economic recovery in East Asia followed a similar pattern. The improvement in trade growth was more evident in value than in volume on account of disparate movements in the prices of internationally traded goods and services in 1998 and 1999. With the major exception of the transition economies, there was a sharp turnaround in all regions, particularly in value terms, as price declines levelled off. As in 1998, Japan experienced particularly sharp swings in both exports and imports, which rose considerably over the previous year. At the same time, the return of financial stability and improved growth prospects in the crisis-stricken Asian economies led to a modest recovery in certain non-oil commodity prices of interest to developing countries.

The expectation for 2000 is for a moderate acceleration in the growth of the volume of world trade, mainly as a result of a somewhat faster growth of the EU economies and economic recovery in Latin America and the transition economies. However, prospects are crucially dependent on developments in the pace and pattern of demand generation, notably in industrial countries, as well as on movements in exchange rates, and hence on international capital flows. While short-term prospects for demand have improved, as noted above, there are serious downside risks due to imbalances on both the real and the financial sides of the global economy, which could induce sharp swings in trade flows, exchange parities and competitiveness and provoke protectionist reactions.

1. Trends in imports and exports

The volume of world imports grew by some 5 per cent in 1999, a modest improvement over 1998, when it slowed sharply as the combined effects of the emerging-market financial crises resulted in massive cuts in imports in East Asia, Latin America and the transition economies (table 3.1). The improvement in 1999 was due mainly to a recovery in developing countries and also to sustained growth in developed countries, albeit at a relatively lower rate than in the previous year; import volumes in the transition economies contracted by 10 per cent.

Table 3.1

EXPORTS AND IMPORTS BY MAJOR REGIONS AND ECONOMIC GROUPINGS, 1996–1999

(Percentage change over previous year)

	Export value				Export volume			
	1996	*1997*	*1998*	*1999*	*1996*	*1997*	*1998*	*1999*
World[a]	5.3	3.5	-1.6	3.5	6.1	10.7	4.7	3.9
Developed market-economy countries	2.9	2.0	0.7	1.7	4.9	10.0	4.3	4.3
of which:								
Japan	-7.3	2.4	-7.8	8.0	1.0	12.0	-1.5	2.0
United States	6.9	10.2	-0.9	1.8	6.3	11.9	2.3	3.2
European Union	3.4	-0.5	3.8	-0.5	5.5	9.5	6.0	3.5
Transition economies	33.9	4.1	-4.6	-1.5	6.5	10.5	5.0	-3.0
Developing countries	7.9	6.9	-6.9	8.3	6.9	12.4	5.6	5.3
of which:								
Africa	14.8	1.9	-15.5	8.0	8.9	6.5	-1.2	3.3
Latin America	12.2	10.2	-1.2	6.0	11.0	11.5	7.5	7.0
Asia	4.5	6.7	-5.1	6.7	5.4	12.5	3.8	7.2
of which:								
Newly industrializing economies[b]	4.3	3.5	-7.5	5.2	9.1	11.6	3.8	5.9
ASEAN-4[c]	5.7	5.0	-3.9	9.9	4.8	12.1	11.0	11.2
China	1.5	21.0	0.6	6.0	-0.8	20.5	3.7	8.3
Memo item:								
ASEAN-4 plus Republic of Korea	4.9	5.0	-3.5	9.5	10.9	17.7	13.7	11.2

	Import value				Import volume			
	1996	*1997*	*1998*	*1999*	*1996*	*1997*	*1998*	*1999*
World[a]	5.8	3.5	-0.8	4.0	6.9	10.0	4.5	5.3
Developed market-economy countries	3.9	2.2	3.3	4.8	5.3	9.3	8.0	6.5
of which:								
Japan	4.0	-3.0	-17.2	11.0	5.5	1.5	-5.5	9.5
United States	6.6	9.4	4.9	12.4	5.6	12.1	11.7	11.5
European Union	2.8	-0.5	6.3	1.0	5.0	8.5	8.5	4.0
Transition economies	48.0	6.5	-1.8	-13.0	16.0	13.5	5.0	-10.0
Developing countries	6.0	6.1	-10.3	4.3	6.4	10.8	-3.8	4.2
of which:								
Africa	-1.1	5.5	1.2	0.5	1.0	9.7	5.3	0.3
Latin America	11.8	18.5	4.8	-4.0	8.5	22.5	8.5	-2.0
Asia	5.1	2.2	-17.3	9.0	5.5	6.7	-9.7	7.3
of which:								
Newly industrializing economies[b]	4.4	3.4	-19.5	7.6	6.6	7.4	-10.0	6.9
ASEAN-4[c]	4.8	-2.5	-27.9	7.8	2.0	5.0	-22.7	9.8
China	5.1	2.5	-1.5	18.0	7.5	5.5	2.3	13.1
Memo item:								
ASEAN-4 plus Republic of Korea	7.3	-3.0	-30.9	15.4	6.3	3.5	-22.0	18.1

Source: WTO Press Release 175, 6 April 2000, tables II.2 and II.3; UNCTAD secretariat calculations, based on data available from WTO.

   a For the (growing) statistical discrepancy between world imports and world exports see text, note 1.
   b Hong Kong (China), Republic of Korea, Singapore and Taiwan Province of China.
   c Indonesia, Malaysia, Philippines and Thailand.

Among the developed countries, the United States economy maintained for the third successive year a double-digit growth in import volumes. There was also a surge in Japan following a decline in 1998. By contrast, there was a significant deceleration in EU. In the developing world performance was also mixed. In Latin America the volume of imports contracted after a relatively rapid expansion in the previous year. In Africa it stagnated, following moderate growth in 1998. For developing Asia, however, there was a sharp upturn from a contraction of almost 10 per cent in 1998 to an increase of some 7 per cent, in large part due to the impressive rebound in East Asia.

Owing to statistical discrepancies, the rebound in world trade in 1999 is not reflected to the same extent in terms of the volume of exports.[1] Indeed, unlike imports, the volume of world exports is estimated to have risen less than in 1998. The slowdown is accounted for by a contraction of exports in the transition economies as well as somewhat slower export growth in developing countries. For developed countries as a whole the export volume growth rate was maintained at the previous year's level. The sharp rebound in Japan, together with continued expansion in the United States, compensated for the deceleration in EU. Among the developing regions, there was a notable rebound in Africa and Asia, in contrast to a moderate slowdown in Latin America.

The dollar value of both world imports and world exports increased in 1999 after contracting in the previous year. The increase was broad-based, with the exception of the transition economies, where both imports and exports fell. There was a relatively rapid increase in the value of imports in the United States and a marked rebound for Japan and for developing Asia. Export earnings increased in all major economic regions except EU and the transition economies.

Differential growth in trade volumes and values reflects changes in unit values. Both world imports and world exports show smaller increases in 1999 in value than in volume terms, on account of price declines. However, the discrepancy between volume and value figures is much narrower for 1999 than for 1998, suggesting that the downward trend in world prices has moderated. In both the United States and Japan, import value growth was higher than volume growth, reflecting in part the impact of rising oil prices. For EU, however, the data show a fall in import unit values despite the decline of the euro, the increase in oil prices and the concern of ECB over their inflationary consequences. For developing countries as a whole changes in import unit values were small on balance. However, while Asia, and to a lesser extent Africa, had rising import prices, in Latin America they fell.

While export prices appear to have risen for the developed countries in general, there are considerable disparities among regions. Japanese export unit values in dollar terms show a significant increase, reflecting in part the appreciation of the yen. By contrast, export unit values in the United States, and even more so in EU, declined. The increase in the unit values of exports of developing countries reflects mainly the impact of sharp increases in oil prices, particularly for Africa; in Asia and Latin America export unit values declined.

Table 3.2 shows changes since 1997 in unit values, volumes and values of exports and imports for selected developing countries in Asia and Latin America, together with the corresponding changes in the terms of trade.[2] After a sharp contraction in 1998, as already noted, import volumes rose considerably in East Asia in 1999, except in Indonesia and Hong Kong (China). The rebound in ASEAN-4, the NIEs and China was particularly impressive. For the crisis-stricken countries taken together (ASEAN-4 and the Republic of Korea), import volumes rose by 18 per cent in 1999, after dropping by more than 20 per cent in 1998. All of these countries managed to raise the volume of their exports in 1998. However, with the exception of the Philippines, their export earnings fell because of falling prices. In 1999, growth in export volumes accelerated in Malaysia and Thailand, and more favourable export prices contributed to sizeable increases in export revenues in all countries affected by the crisis, except Indonesia. Over the past three years the terms of trade have been stable or moving against most Asian countries included in table 3.2. Overall, Indonesia suffered the largest terms-of-trade losses, followed by the Republic of Korea, Malaysia and India.

Although exports from Latin America as a whole increased by 6–7 per cent in 1999, this outcome was due primarily to Mexico, where the increase was some 16 per cent in value and 13 per cent in volume. Indeed, export earnings for the rest of the region were lower than the previous year. The failure of most Latin American coun-

Table 3.2

FOREIGN TRADE AND THE TERMS OF TRADE OF SELECTED DEVELOPING ECONOMIES, 1998–1999

(Percentage change over previous year)

Economy	Exports						Imports						Terms of trade		
	Volume		Unit value		Value		Volume		Unit value		Value				
	1998	1999	1998	1999	1998	1999	1998	1999	1998	1999	1998	1999	1997	1998	1999
Asia															
Hong Kong, China	-4.3	2.6	-2.9	-2.6	-7.1	-0.1	-7.1	-1.2	-5.8	-1.5	-12.4	-2.7	-0.8	3.0	-1.1
Republic of Korea	16.9	11.3	-16.9	-2.1	-2.8	9.0	-21.0	29.3	-18.4	-0.7	-35.5	28.3	-11.3	1.8	-1.4
Singapore	-0.7	3.5	-11.4	0.8	-12.1	4.3	-12.7	2.0	-12.3	7.2	-23.4	9.4	0.4	0.9	-6.0
Taiwan Province of China	1.1	3.3	-9.7	6.5	-8.7	10.1	4.1	1.2	-11.5	4.6	-7.9	5.8	0.9	2.0	1.9
Indonesia	17.2	-1.7	-22.0	1.0	-8.6	-0.7	-30.8	-11.7	-5.2	-1.0	-34.4	-12.5	1.6	-17.7	2.0
Malaysia	3.9	20.0	-10.4	-3.9	-6.9	15.3	-21.2	14.4	-6.3	-1.8	-26.2	12.3	-0.2	-4.4	-2.1
Philippines	24.8	18.7	-5.3	0.1	18.2	18.8	-13.9	3.5	-5.3	0.1	-18.4	3.6	0.0	0.0	0.0
Thailand	7.9	9.8	-12.1	-2.3	-5.1	7.3	-25.7	24.4	-8.0	-5.4	-31.6	17.6	-1.5	-4.4	3.3
India	-0.5	12.0	-3.4	-3.0	-3.9	8.7	12.2	0.2	-8.0	4.1	3.2	4.3	-3.6	5.0	-6.8
China	3.7	8.3	-3.0	-2.1	0.6	6.0	2.3	13.1	-3.7	4.5	-1.5	18.2	3.3	0.7	-6.3
Latin America [a]															
Argentina	9.9	-5.0	-9.0	-8.0	0.0	-12.6	8.1	-14.4	-4.6	-5.0	3.1	-18.6	0.4	-4.6	-3.2
Brazil	4.6	2.9	-8.0	-10.0	-3.8	-7.5	2.7	-13.0	-6.0	-2.0	-3.5	-14.7	5.7	-2.1	-8.2
Chile	8.0	11.3	-17.6	-7.0	-11.1	3.6	-0.2	-13.0	-4.6	-2.5	-4.7	-15.3	3.8	-13.6	-4.5
Colombia	7.1	6.3	-12.0	2.4	-5.8	9.0	-0.7	-28.0	-4.5	-2.5	-5.2	-29.8	9.8	-8.0	5.1
Ecuador	-5.5	0.4	-15.5	2.0	-20.1	2.4	17.2	-50.6	-5.0	-2.5	11.4	-51.8	2.1	-11.0	4.5
Mexico	10.8	13.1	-4.0	2.5	6.4	16.0	16.0	14.2	-1.6	-1.5	14.1	12.6	-0.8	-2.5	4.0
Peru	1.3	17.2	-17.1	-10.0	-16.0	5.6	0.4	-17.4	-4.6	-1.0	-4.1	-18.2	6.9	-13.1	-9.1
Venezuela	1.4	-5.7	-27.1	24.0	-26.0	16.9	9.5	-11.7	-1.5	-2.5	7.8	-14.0	-3.1	-25.9	27.1

Source: UNCTAD secretariat calculations, based on statistics of WTO and national sources.

   a Figures for 1999 are preliminary, based on ECLAC, *Preliminary Overview of the Economies of Latin America and the Caribbean, 1999*, United Nations publication, sales no. E.99.II.G.58, Santiago, Chile, 1999, tables A-8, A-9 and A-10.

Table 3.3

INTRA-ASIAN TRADE, 1996–1998

Regional sub-group[a]	Year	Exports				Imports			
		Value ($ billion)	Percentage change	Percentage of Group exports	Percentage of World exports	Value ($ billion)	Percentage change	Percentage of Group imports	Percentage of World imports
Asia-8	1996	198.7	6.1	33.0	4.0	180.6	6.1	22.2	3.5
	1997	205.8	3.6	32.9	4.0	184.2	2.0	22.3	3.4
	1998	175.3	-14.8	30.0	3.5	148.4	-19.5	23.0	2.8
Asia-9	1996	280.2	4.5	37.2	5.7	323.5	6.6	34.0	6.2
	1997	305.7	9.1	37.8	5.9	339.4	4.9	35.0	6.3
	1998	263.3	-13.9	34.3	5.2	293.8	-13.4	37.4	5.5
Asia-10	1996	563.1	1.0	48.4	11.4	641.2	2.7	49.3	12.3
	1997	582.9	3.5	47.4	11.3	646.2	0.8	49.4	11.9
	1998	484.3	-16.9	41.9	9.5	538.3	-16.7	50.5	10.1

Source: UNCTAD secretariat calculations, based on data from the United Nations Compressed International Commodity Trade Data Base (COMTRADE).

a Asia-8: the four Asian NIEs (Hong Kong, China; Republic of Korea; Singapore and Taiwan Province of China) and ASEAN-4 (Indonesia, Malaysia, Philippines, Thailand); Asia-9: Asia-8 plus China; Asia-10: Asia-9 plus Japan.

tries to generate higher export earnings, in spite of competitive gains from currency devaluation, is attributable in part to weak world commodity markets, inasmuch as countries in the region continue to be major commodity exporters, and in part to the collapse in intraregional trade by some 25 per cent during the first three quarters of 1999, following its first contraction for 12 years in 1998. The decline in export unit values either more than offset the increase in volume (e.g. Brazil and Guatemala) or was accompanied by a fall in export volume (e.g. Argentina, Bolivia, Honduras, Panama, Paraguay and Uruguay). The decline in export earnings largely explains why the overall value of merchandise imports of Latin America declined in 1999 for the first time in 15 years, despite the substantial increase for Mexico.

2. Intraregional trade in East Asia

Trade played an important role in the build-up of external fragility and the outbreak of the financial crisis, as well as in the subsequent recovery, in East Asia. From the mid-1990s declines in export prices and slower growth in export earnings resulted in a widening of trade deficits and contributed to the loss of investor confidence.[3] Strong intraregional trade linkages[4] were an important factor in regional contagion, particularly since exchange-rate stability was an essential ingredient of regional integration. However, the same interdependence has also worked to reinforce the growth impulses during the current recovery. While strong growth of the United States economy, the region's most important export market, together with increased competitiveness brought about by currency devaluations, provided an independent export stimulus, intraregional trade linkages have acted to amplify the growth impulses through a multiplier effect.

Table 3.3 shows intra-Asian trade in 1996–1998 for three alternative country groupings: "Asia-8" comprising the four Asian NIEs and ASEAN-4; "Asia-9" (Asia-8 plus China) and "Asia-10" (Asia-9 plus Japan). The relative importance of intraregional exports and imports in each group is indicated by its share in total exports and imports of the group as well as by its share in the corresponding world aggregate.

Table 3.4

GEOGRAPHICAL DISTRIBUTION OF EXPORTS OF SELECTED
ASIAN COUNTRIES AND COUNTRY GROUPS, 1995–1998

(Percentage share in total exports)

Exports from		Destination of exports					
		United States	European Union	Japan	NIEs	ASEAN-4	China
Japan	1995	27.5	15.9	-	25.0	12.1	5.0
	1996	27.5	15.4	-	24.7	12.4	5.3
	1997	28.1	15.6	-	24.0	11.4	5.2
	1998	30.9	18.5	-	20.2	7.8	5.2
NIEs	1995	20.9	13.5	10.6	19.6	13.5	5.3
	1996	19.8	13.1	10.3	19.6	13.8	5.9
	1997	19.6	13.6	9.6	19.9	13.3	6.5
	1998	20.6	14.7	8.8	18.3	11.4	6.3
Republic of Korea	1995	19.5	13.0	13.6	17.0	7.9	7.3
	1996	16.9	11.9	12.2	16.6	9.3	8.8
	1997	16.0	12.4	10.8	16.3	9.4	10.0
	1998	17.4	13.8	9.2	14.0	7.3	9.0
ASEAN-4	1995	19.7	14.9	17.5	25.5	5.6	2.9
	1996	18.6	15.2	17.9	25.9	6.5	3.0
	1997	19.5	15.5	16.3	25.7	6.7	2.8
	1998	21.2	16.7	14.2	24.0	6.6	2.8
China	1995	16.6	12.9	19.1	33.1	3.7	-
	1996	17.7	13.1	20.4	31.1	3.4	-
	1997	17.9	13.1	17.4	33.2	3.6	-
	1998	20.7	15.3	16.1	28.7	3.0	-

Source: See table 3.3.

The intraregional trade of Asia-10 accounted for almost 50 per cent of the group's total trade and around 12 per cent of total world trade prior to the Asian crisis. Both intraregional exports and intraregional imports fell by some 17 per cent in 1998 as the crisis deepened, and their shares in total world exports and imports dropped to some 10 per cent. Indeed, the collapse in intra-Asian trade in 1998 was a major cause of the slump in world trade.[5] Much of the decline was due to contraction in the dollar value of Japanese imports and exports, as noted above. However, the group including only the developing countries and China (Asia-9) also suffered from a significant loss of intraregional exports and imports during 1998.

Table 3.4 compares the distribution of exports of selected Asian countries and country groupings among various destinations within and outside the region. Clearly, outside the region, the United States is the most important market for the exports of East Asian countries, including both China and Japan. Dependence on the United States market is similar for NIEs, ASEAN-4 and China, but somewhat greater for Japan. Before the outbreak of the crisis, the importance of East Asian developing countries for Japanese exports was similar to that of the United States and EU taken together, while the NIEs have always been significantly more important than EU. Similarly, for China the importance of the NIEs outweighs that of Japan, the United States or EU. Among the developing countries, intraregional exports are more important for the NIEs than for ASEAN-4. For the NIEs, the share of intra-group trade in its total exports is almost the same as the share of its exports to the United States, and significantly greater than that of its exports to EU or ASEAN-4. For ASEAN-4, the NIEs are more important as export markets than the United States or EU.

For all the East Asian countries in table 3.4, the share of exports to destinations outside the region rose with the deepening of the crisis in 1998. Since, as already noted, total export earnings of the developing countries of the region (except China) fell, this reflects the sharp drop in intraregional trade rather than an absolute increase in exports to the United States or Europe. Although comparable figures are not available for the more recent period of recovery, it appears that intraregional trade has been reviving as much as trade with countries outside the region.

B. Non-oil commodity markets

In 1999, world commodity markets continued to suffer from the lingering effects of the economic slowdown of the previous year, which reduced demand and exerted a downward pressure on the prices of most commodities. There was some recovery in world demand, but commodity prices failed to pick up strongly owing to a large stock overhang. The downward trend in most prices levelled off by mid-1999 and prices have since increased moderately. However, they are yet to recover from the marked slump in the aftermath of the Asian and Brazilian crises, which lasted for over two years and resulted in a decline in the commodity price index (excluding crude petroleum) of about 30 per cent. The persistent and precipitous fall in prices in 1998 and 1999 affected all major commodity groups, including food and tropical beverages, agricultural raw materials, and minerals, ores and metals. The only exceptions are vegetable oilseeds and oils, the prices of which had increased by 7 per cent in 1998, but fell sharply in 1999 (table 3.5).

The pronounced widespread decline in non-oil commodity prices in both 1998 and 1999 reflects a combination of sluggish demand and ample supplies in almost all markets. It also reflects the continued effects of currency devaluations for important commodity exporters and importers, most notably Brazil and the Russian Federation. The large devaluations in Brazil led to a marked increase in exports of sugar and coffee, whereas the devaluation of the Russian rouble reduced the demand for many imported commodities. The decline in world demand for many non-oil commodities has been brought about mainly by the sharp economic downturn experienced in most East Asian countries. At the same time, technological advances have enhanced productivity and reduced production costs in many cases, leading to an oversupply in commodity markets. Furthermore, novel applications of genetic engineering and biotechnology in agriculture, combined with favourable weather conditions, have resulted in significantly higher output of most agricultural products.

Notwithstanding the improvement in the global economy, which boosted commodity demand in the second half of 1999, prices of non-oil primary commodities for the year as a whole were on average well below the 1998 level. The fall of over 14 per cent was the largest since 1982 (over 21 per cent) and pushed the index of non-oil primary commodities to its lowest level since 1985. The fall was widespread among commodities, but the collapse in sugar and cocoa prices by 30 per cent and 32 per cent, respectively, was particularly acute. Coffee and cotton prices dropped by more than 20 per cent, those of wheat, rice and rubber by more than 10 per cent, and tea, maize, bananas, tobacco, tropical logs and ores by more than 5 per cent.

With cyclical lows now past for most commodities, the outlook for the current year is for some price revival, particularly for industrial materials and metals, but food prices are expected to

Table 3.5

WORLD PRIMARY COMMODITY PRICES, 1996–2000

(Percentage change over previous year)

Commodity group	1996	1997	1998	1999	April 2000[a]
All commodities[b]	**-4.2**	**0.0**	**-13.0**	**-14.2**	**-1.0**
Food and tropical beverages	**2.1**	**2.8**	**-14.3**	**-18.3**	**-1.0**
Tropical beverages	-15.2	33.3	-17.3	-20.9	-16.2
Coffee	-19.1	54.7	-28.5	-23.2	-24.0
Cocoa	1.2	11.2	3.7	-32.1	-0.8
Tea[c]	...	35.1	4.3	-7.0	9.1
Food	6.8	-3.5	-13.8	-18.1	3.5
Sugar	-9.9	-4.9	-21.2	-30.0	0.2
Beef	-6.4	4.0	-7.0	6.1	1.3
Maize	25.0	-25.3	-13.4	-5.5	7.6
Wheat	16.2	-22.6	-19.9	-10.9	4.7
Rice	5.0	-10.7	1.3	-18.6	-6.1
Bananas	7.5	4.3	-3.1	-9.9	24.3
Vegetable oilseeds and oils	**-4.2**	**-0.9**	**7.1**	**-23.3**	**0.0**
Agricultural raw materials	**-9.9**	**-10.3**	**-10.8**	**-10.3**	**1.0**
Hides and skins	-23.7	-19.8	-22.7	-27.6	-0.9
Cotton	-14.8	-8.9	-8.3	-22.9	36.7
Tobacco	15.6	15.6	-5.5	-7.0	-3.4
Rubber	-11.9	-28.3	-29.8	-12.6	7.8
Tropical logs	-20.1	-5.5	-1.2	-7.2	-6.4
Minerals, ores and metals	**-12.1**	**0.0**	**-16.0**	**-1.8**	**-0.8**
Aluminium	-16.6	6.2	-15.1	0.3	-6.3
Phosphate rock	8.6	7.9	2.4	4.6	0.0
Iron ore	6.0	1.1	2.8	-9.2	2.6
Tin	-0.8	-8.4	-1.9	-2.5	-5.9
Copper	-21.8	-0.8	-27.3	-4.9	-4.9
Nickel	-8.8	-7.6	-33.2	29.8	20.3
Tungsten ore	-17.9	-9.3	-6.4	-9.3	2.3
Lead	22.7	-19.4	-15.3	-5.0	-12.1
Zinc	-0.6	28.4	-22.2	5.1	-4.7

Source: UNCTAD, *Monthly Commodity Price Bulletin,* various issues.
> *a* Change from December 1999.
> *b* Excluding crude petroleum.
> *c* New series, with data starting in 1996.

remain low. In April 2000 average prices of non-oil commodities were only 1 per cent lower than in December 1999. However, there was variation among commodities. For example, prices for cotton, bananas and nickel rose by about 37 per cent, 24 per cent and 20 per cent, respectively, during those four months, but those of coffee and lead fell by 24 per cent and 12 per cent, respectively. Price variations for agricultural commodities, reflecting changes in stock levels, have been particularly pronounced and are expected to continue for the remainder of the year. Overall, prices of food and tropical beverages are expected to remain depressed as production continues to outstrip demand for coffee, sugar and vegetable oilseeds. However, prices of some agricultural raw materials and minerals, ores and metals are expected to continue to increase, owing to the impact of renewed economic growth in Asia and strong housing demand in the United States.

C. Recent developments and emerging trends in oil markets

1. Prices, production and demand

The key feature of the oil market in 1999 was the sharp rise in crude oil prices to unexpectedly high levels (chart 3.1). After falling almost continuously throughout 1998 and dropping below $10 a barrel in early 1999, crude oil prices[6] rebounded steadily throughout the year, so that prices averaged $17.5 a barrel for the year as a whole. The increase is more remarkable when the price at the beginning of 1999 ($10.5) is compared with that at the end of the year ($25). The rally in oil prices in 1999 accounted for about $75 billion (some 40 per cent) of the increase in world merchandise exports.

Oil prices rose sharply after OPEC and non-OPEC producers (Mexico, Norway, Oman and the Russian Federation) had jointly decided to cut output by 2.1 million barrels per day (bpd) as of 1 April 1999. These production cuts, in addition to those pledged by OPEC in 1998, amounted to an overall reduction of 4.7 million bpd, or 6 per cent of world oil supply. They coincided with strengthening demand for oil associated with the economic recovery in Asia, one of the world's most important sources of incremental demand prior to 1998. They also came at a time of continued strong growth in the United States economy and when supply from non-OPEC producers was rising much less rapidly than demand. The combination of all these factors has led to a depletion of world oil stockpiles to a very low level.

The most notable feature of the agreement was not so much the level of the announced cuts as the unusually firm commitment to production quotas, compliance with which has averaged about 85 per cent.[7] Unlike in past years, and in spite of improved market conditions, OPEC members have resisted the temptation to produce more oil in the face of rising demand and prices. The reason for this unusually high level of compliance was a disturbing and painful earlier episode of very low oil prices and revenues. For about 15 months, during January 1998–March 1999, oil-exporting countries had seen their oil revenues drop by over one third to their lowest level since 1972, despite a marked increase in the volume exported. Many of them suffered seriously, as their infrastructure, manufacturing and social services bore the consequences of severe budgetary cuts.

Following OPEC's decision in September 1999 to maintain supply limits until March 2000,

Chart 3.1

MONTHLY AVERAGE SPOT PRICES OF OPEC CRUDE OILS,[a] JANUARY 1998 TO MAY 2000

(Dollars per barrel)

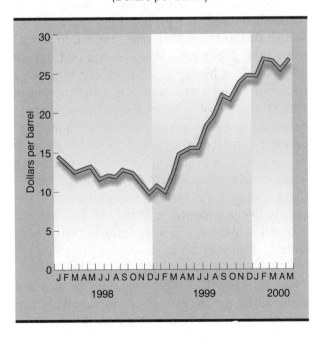

Source: OPEC.
a Average spot prices of the basket of seven OPEC crude oils.

Chart 3.2

OIL EXPORT REVENUES OF OPEC PRODUCERS IN 1998 AND 1999

(Billions of dollars)

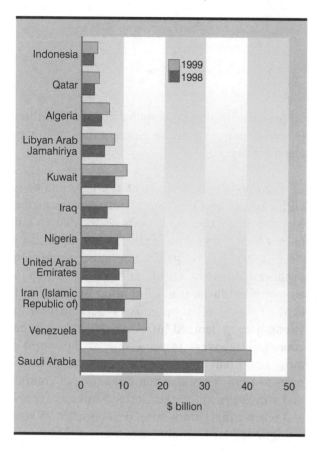

Source: 1998: OPEC; 1999: UNCTAD secretariat estimates.

prices was also helped by anxiety about the availability of reformulated gasoline supplies in the United States in the run-up to the summer driving season.

The sudden increase in prices has been a boon for the major oil exporters and significantly improved their terms of trade. For example, OPEC oil revenues in 1999 are estimated to have risen to about $138 billion, an increase of 36 per cent over 1998 (see chart 3.2 for country detail). Other major oil exporters, such as Mexico, Norway, Oman and the Russian Federation, also benefited considerably. While oil-exporting countries have thus recovered much of the revenues lost in 1998, the major consuming countries have expressed concern over the potentially adverse effects on growth and inflation of the price hikes. However, the impact on inflation has remained relatively small: in the United States, for example, the $5.2 per barrel increase in the annual average price in 1999 is estimated to have contributed to an increase of some 0.3 per cent in inflation.[8] Similarly, various simulations undertaken in UNCTAD and other international organizations suggest that the impact of rising oil prices on global growth will be limited, and confined mostly to oil-importing developing countries (see box 3.1). However, little attention has been given to the plea of financially strained, low-income, oil-importing developing countries, whose balance of payments have deteriorated significantly on account of oil.

Despite the sharp increase in prices, world oil demand rose by 1.5 per cent in 1999 (table 3.6). While this is a modest rate, compared to the more than 2 per cent average attained during 1995–1997, it has been accompanied by a large depletion of oil inventories. Oil consumption in OECD countries was led by North America, where demand rose by 3.0 per cent. In the developed Pacific countries it grew by 2.3 per cent. The increase in demand in developing countries (excluding Mexico and the Republic of Korea) was also above the world average, owing mainly to a strong recovery in consumption in East Asia. By contrast, demand in Western Europe contracted slightly in spite of relatively strong economic growth.

The growth in demand in 1999 was not matched by an increase in world supply, which fell by 1.4 million bpd (1.9 per cent) because of the agreements on output cutbacks referred to above (table 3.7). The shortfall was met from oil stocks, which are estimated to have declined by

prices continued to rise, reaching $27 a barrel in February, before falling slightly in anticipation of a decision to allow some increases in output at the OPEC meeting scheduled for the end of March. At that meeting, OPEC agreed to raise output by 1.45 million bpd, starting on 1 April 2000. An additional aggregate production increase of about 0.5 million bpd was later announced by the Islamic Republic of Iran, Mexico and Norway. At the same meeting, OPEC members informally endorsed an output-varying scheme aimed at preventing oil prices from emerging from the range $22–$28 a barrel, raising output if prices rose above $28 and reducing it if they fell below $22. After the meeting prices fell temporarily and then bounced back to about $27 a barrel in May 2000. The view of markets was that the extra output was not enough to rebuild oil stocks sufficiently to keep prices at more moderate levels. The rise in

IMPACT OF OIL PRICES ON WORLD OUTPUT

The continued rise in oil prices since March 1999 has given rise to growing concern that the world economy could undergo another oil shock similar to that of the 1970s. To provide some indications of the impact of an increase in oil prices on output growth in the immediate and longer term, a simulation exercise has been carried out which assumes an increase in the price of oil from a baseline level of $26 per barrel in 2000 to $31 in the future.[1] In the system, the equation for the price of oil is specified to be dependent on the export prices of industrialized countries as well as on the ratio of oil consumption to energy requirements at the global level, with a one-year lag for both variables. At the same time, the increase in oil prices induces greater energy conservation and greater utilization of alternative energy sources, thus reducing the oil intensity of output, as experienced in the United States in recent years. As a consequence, the price of oil, instead of remaining at this higher level during the entire simulation period, is projected to decline gradually to less than $29 per barrel by 2015.

Simulation results associated with the specified increase in oil prices in 2000 are expressed as changes in the rates of GDP growth over those of the baseline for the years 2000–2015. Because of the specification of a one-year lag in the explanatory variables in the equation for both oil prices and oil requirements at the country and subregional levels, the immediate impact of the price increase in oil is generally marginal in 2000, with the notable exceptions of the Philippines and Thailand (-0.3 of a percentage point).

Over the longer term, the impact on growth is much more significant in the five years starting in 2010 than in earlier periods, and will be felt more in developing countries than in developed countries. In the immediate future (2000–2005), the impact is greatest in the Middle East (1.0 percentage point), but is also significant for Indonesia, the Philippines and Thailand (-0.3 to -0.4 of a percentage point), and least for Singapore and the Republic of Korea (-0.2 of a percentage point). For oil exporters, especially those in the Middle East, the longer-term impact of higher oil prices on growth is expected to be negative because sustaining higher prices will necessitate reductions in oil output.

Similar simulations have been carried out by other institutions. Although comparisons cannot always be made because of differences in assumptions underlying the baseline scenarios and the use of different global modelling systems, in general they reach similar conclusions. OECD, for example, assumes an increase in oil prices of $10 per barrel (presumably over the baseline, based on an average of $22 per barrel for the first half of 2000).[2] The outcome relative to the baseline is a loss of 0.2 of a percentage point in GDP growth for both the United States and EU, and a greater loss (0.4 of a percentage point) for Japan because of its greater dependence on oil imports. In the IMF simulation, which assumes a 10 per cent increase in the price of oil from a baseline level of $18 per barrel in 2000, the loss in output is 0.1 of a percentage point individually for the United States, Japan and the euro area.[3] In the World Bank scenario, which assumes an oil price of $30 per barrel in 2000 and $25 per barrel in 2001, as compared respectively to $23 per barrel and $19 per barrel in the baseline, the loss in world output amounts to 0.2 of a percentage point in 2000 and 0.4 of a percentage point in 2001.[4]

---

[1] The UNCTAD secretariat is grateful to Akira Onishi, Vice-President of Soka University, for carrying out both the baseline projections and the oil price scenario using the FUGI Global Model 9.0 M200. For a detailed description of the FUGI global model, including its historical background, methodology, scope and structure, see Onishi A, *FUGI Global Model 9.0 M200/80: Integrated Global Model for Sustainable Development*, Soka University, Institute of Systems Science, Tokyo, 31 March 1999.

[2] *OECD Economic Outlook*, Dec. 1999.

[3] IMF, *World Economic Outlook*, Oct. 1999.

[4] World Bank, *Global Development Finance 2000*, Washington, DC, World Bank, May 2000, box 1.2.

Table 3.6

WORLD OIL DEMAND BY REGION, 1996–1999 [a]

(Millions of barrels per day)

	1996	1997	1998	1999
OECD	45.9	46.7	46.8	47.5
North America	22.2	22.7	23.1	23.8
Europe	14.9	15.0	15.3	15.1
Pacific [b]	8.8	9.0	8.4	8.6
Other countries	25.7	26.8	27.1	27.5
Central and Eastern Europe [c]	0.8	0.8	0.8	0.8
Former Soviet Union [d]	4.3	4.3	4.1	4.0
Developing countries [e]	20.6	21.7	22.3	22.7
Latin America	4.3	4.4	4.6	4.6
Africa	2.2	2.3	2.4	2.4
West Asia	4.0	4.2	4.3	4.2
South and East Asia	6.4	6.7	6.8	7.1
China [d]	3.7	4.1	4.2	4.4
World total	71.6	73.4	73.9	75.0

Source: International Energy Agency, *Monthly Oil Market Report*, various issues.

  a Including deliveries from refineries/primary stocks and marine bunkers, and refinery fuel and non-conventional oils.
  b Australia, Japan, New Zealand and Republic of Korea.
  c Excluding the Czech Republic and Hungary.
  d Based on estimates of apparent domestic demand derived from official production figures and quarterly trade data.
  e Excluding Mexico and Republic of Korea.

nearly 1 million bpd after having been replenished at a rate of 1.6 million bpd in 1998. A much higher rate of stock depletion (about 1.7 million bpd) occurred in the first quarter of 2000 as a result of increased demand brought about by the cold winter in North America.

2. The uncertain outlook

The outlook for oil prices is highly uncertain. The key factors responsible for strong price increases in 1999 – greater harmony among most OPEC members, rising oil demand brought about by the rapid economic recovery in East Asia and continued expansion in the United States – still prevail. Prices have resumed a sharp rise, pulling the market into "backwardation"[9] as oil stockpiles continued to be depleted.

Should OPEC members opt to maintain their production ceiling at its current level, oil prices will remain well above $20 a barrel. However, it is not certain that prices at that level can be sustained for long. Most oil-exporting countries recognize that a prolonged period of excessively high prices is prejudicial to their own interests, since it reduces demand for oil, stimulates investment in high-cost oil fields, brings additional non-OPEC

Table 3.7

WORLD OIL PRODUCTION BY REGION, 1990–1999 [a]

(Millions of barrels per day)

Country/region	1990	1995	1996	1997	1998	1999
Developed countries	15.9	18.0	18.7	19.1	18.8	18.1
Transition economies	11.8	7.4	7.5	7.4	7.5	7.5
Developing countries	38.0	43.1	44.4	46.4	47.4	46.7
OPEC [b]	25.1	27.7	28.5	30.0	30.7	29.5
Other [c]	12.9	15.3	15.9	16.4	16.7	17.2
Processing gains [d]	1.3	1.5	1.5	1.6	1.6	1.7
World total	67.0	70.0	72.0	74.1	75.4	74.0

Source: UNCTAD secretariat estimates, based on International Energy Agency, *Monthly Oil Market Report*, various issues.

  a Crude oil, condensates, natural gas liquids, oil from non-conventional sources and other sources of supply.
  b Including Ecuador up to 1992 and Gabon up to 1994.
  c Including Ecuador from 1993 and Gabon from 1995.
  d Net volumetric gains and losses in refining process (excludes net gain/loss in the economies in transition and China) and marine transportation losses.

supply on stream, and encourages substitution of alternative sources of energy.

With demand and supply tightly balanced and inventories low, the oil market remains potentially volatile. In order to prevent prices from rising further, an increase in output from OPEC in 2000 will be needed. At its meeting in June, OPEC unanimously agreed to raise output by about 0.7 million bpd, and Mexico and Norway are expected to contribute another 0.2 million bpd. These increments, amounting to just over 1 per cent of world oil consumption, were not enough to impress the market and relieve the pressure on prices.

There are accordingly expectations that at its meeting in September OPEC will decide to raise the production ceiling further in order to avoid the substantial negative repercussions described above. Thus, OPEC output is expected to rise gradually in the coming months, whether through increased quotas or through weaker quota compliance by member countries. Already, oil prices fell slightly in early July following the announcement of the unilateral decision of Saudi Arabia to increase production by 0.5 million bpd. Largely for these reasons, oil prices in the second half of the year are expected to decline moderately and thus to average $24 a barrel for the year as a whole.

D. Currency markets and policy responses in major emerging markets

1999 was a less turbulent year than 1998 for the currencies of major emerging-market economies. The currency regimes of these economies continued to span the spectrum from rigid pegs (Argentina and Hong Kong, China) through various forms of managed floating to full flexibility. The period was marked by widespread easing of monetary conditions in these economies. Substantial movements in exchange rates were rare in East Asian countries but more frequent elsewhere.

Outside East and South Asia, 1999 and the early part of 2000 witnessed some movement towards greater flexibility of exchange rates. In Latin America, Brazil relinquished the band for the real/dollar exchange rate for free floating in January 1999 as part of the response to its currency crisis. Subsequently Chile and Colombia also shifted from currency-band regimes to floating.[10] In Central and Eastern Europe, Poland abandoned in April 2000 a broad band for the zloty in favour of a freer float, but the new currency regime is likely still to be characterized by official intervention to influence the exchange rate in certain circumstances.[11] In East Asia, by contrast, the Republic of Korea has moved away from the free-floating regime introduced during the region's financial crisis towards "dirtier" floating, in which the central bank intervenes in the foreign-

exchange market at the direction of the Ministry of Finance.[12] Malaysia maintained the exchange rate for the ringgit at the level established in September 1998, in conjunction with a programme of capital controls designed to eliminate off-shore speculative trading in the ringgit (see box 4.1 below). In February 1999 the restrictions on capital repatriation by non-resident portfolio investors were relaxed, being replaced for existing investors by a tax varying according to the length of the period during which the assets were held and for new investors by a tax on capital gains, also varying with the holding period. Between the beginning of September 1999, the earliest date on which investments by non-residents could be repatriated without incurring the exit tax, and the end of the year the net outflow of portfolio investment from Malaysia has been moderate.[13]

In East Asia the trend in monetary conditions in 1999 was towards greater ease, with the principal exceptions of Singapore and Taiwan Province of China, two economies which had been less affected by the region's financial crisis, as well as Hong Kong (China), where the rigid link of the currency to the United States dollar leaves its economy more exposed to changes in external monetary conditions (see chart 3.3). The easing of conditions was associated for the most part with

Chart 3.3

EXCHANGE RATES AND MONEY-MARKET RATES IN SELECTED EMERGING-MARKET ECONOMIES, JANUARY 1998 TO APRIL 2000

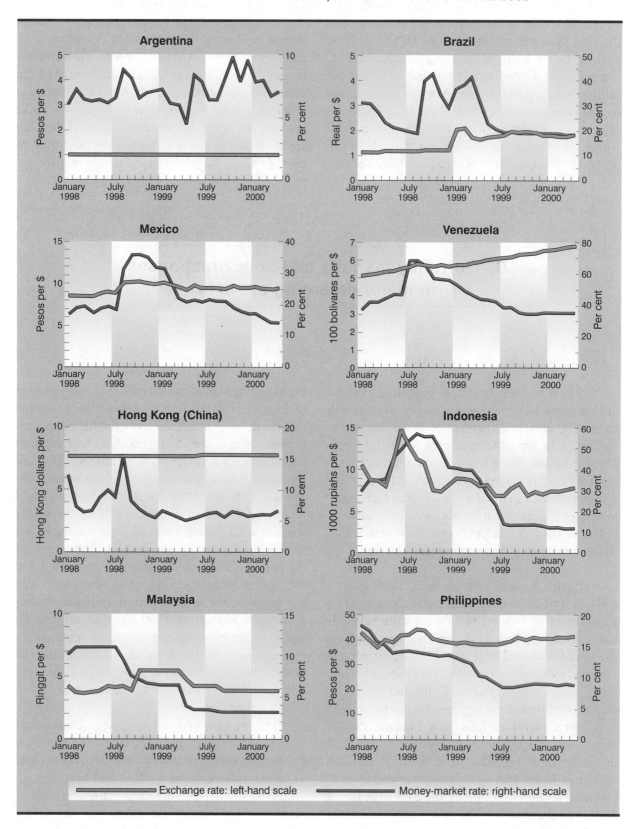

Chart 3.3 (concluded)

EXCHANGE RATES AND MONEY-MARKET RATES IN SELECTED EMERGING-MARKET ECONOMIES, JANUARY 1998 TO APRIL 2000

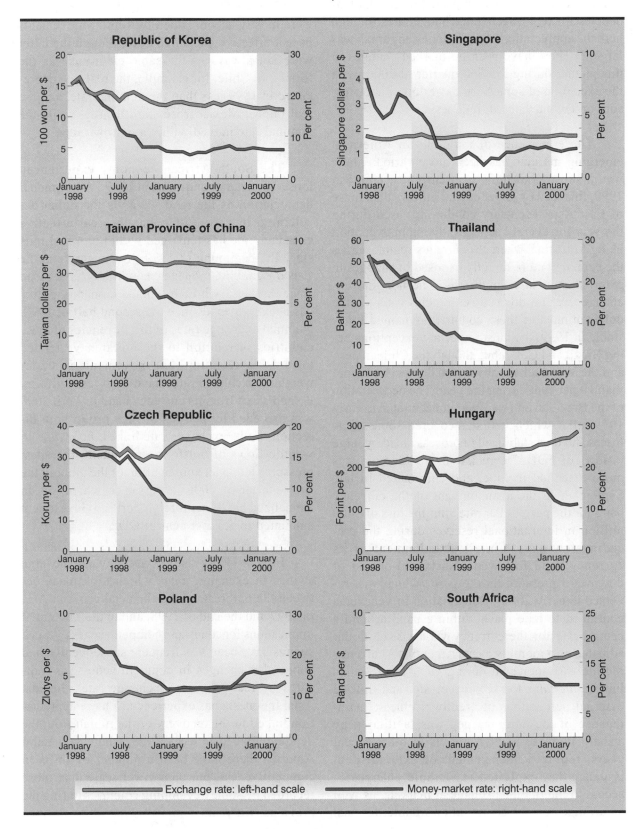

Exchange rate: left-hand scale   Money-market rate: right-hand scale

Source: Primark Datastream; JP Morgan, *Global Data Watch*, various issues.

Note: Argentina, Brazil, Mexico, Indonesia, Malaysia, Philippines, Republic of Korea, Thailand, Czech Republic, Hungary and Poland: three-month domestic money-market rates or nearest equivalent; Venezuela: average lending middle rate; South Africa: discount three-month middle rate; Taiwan Province of China: money-market 90-day-middle rate; Hong Kong (China) and Singapore: interbank three-month middle rate.

greater stability in nominal exchange rates than during the previous two years, but with significant currency appreciation in Indonesia and the Republic of Korea (see chart 3.3). The stability of nominal rates was accompanied by similar tendencies for real effective exchange rates, though here the appreciation of the Indonesian rupiah was larger.[14] There have been no marked changes in this picture during the first quarter of 2000, with the exception of some periods of downward pressure on the currency in Indonesia.

The experience of major Latin American emerging markets has been more varied. There was a substantial deficit on current account in 1999, financed by larger capital inflows than those of East Asia. Monetary conditions eased during the year in several countries, the main exception being Argentina, where the currency regime leaves the economy more directly exposed to changes in external monetary conditions. The nominal exchange rates for domestic currencies vis-à-vis the dollar in most of these countries remained fairly stable in 1999, the most important exceptions being Brazil and Colombia, though the Chilean peso and the Venezuelan bolivar also depreciated more than 10 per cent during the year. The depreciation of the Brazilian currency was concentrated in early 1999, after which it first recovered some of its losses and then stabilized (a process aided by large inflows of FDI). Depreciation in Colombia was more extended in time, and culminated in late September in the abandonment of the currency band for the peso/dollar rate after the loss of $400 million in international reserves during the preceding few days. Chile's abandonment of its currency band followed a sustained period of downward pressure on the peso (which was reversed in early 2000). Depreciation in Venezuela continued to take place within a band around a central rate for the currency vis-à-vis the dollar adjusted on a monthly basis. Argentina's currency regime was subjected during 1999 to pressures linked, *inter alia*, to a severe recession and shifting external perceptions of creditworthiness; maintenance of the currency peg was facilitated by a sharp increase in FDI and, as in other recent years, required management of external debt issuance that exploited favourable changes in access to international financial markets, as well as arrangement or continuation of international

financial facilities from both banks and multilateral lenders which would serve as a safety net in the event of large capital outflows.

These changes in nominal exchange rates were mostly accompanied by similar movements in real effective exchange rates, though the latter were not always of the same magnitude as the former. In Chile, for example, the real rate depreciated in 1999 less than the nominal rate, and the real rate in Mexico rose significantly, while the nominal rate moved within a narrow range.

The South African economy experienced looser monetary conditions in 1999.[15] The gradual depreciation of the rand vis-à-vis the dollar accelerated in early 2000, but the real effective exchange rate has remained within narrow limits since the beginning of 1999. In Hungary and the Czech Republic, monetary conditions have eased since that date, whilst in Poland monetary policy has been tightened since the second half of 1999. Nominal exchange rates of the currencies of these countries in relation to the dollar have tended towards depreciation, but movements in trade-weighted exchange rates have been less uniform. Poland's exit from its currency band in April 2000 was preceded by periods of pressure in both directions on its exchange rate linked, *inter alia*, to volatile flows of portfolio investment; the latest pressures led to an appreciation of the zloty in the first quarter of 2000, a period in which, on an annualized basis, net foreign portfolio investment amounted to 5.5. per cent of GDP.[16]

In *TDR 1999* attention was drawn to the large swings in exchange rates which took place between the outbreak of the financial crisis in Asia in 1997 and the end of 1998, and to their potential implications for countries' competitiveness.[17] Such swings have been less frequent subsequently, and hence also changes in competitiveness, as indicated by real effective exchange rates. In East Asia, Indonesia has experienced a large appreciation linked to the recovery of the rupiah from the depths plumbed in early 1998, whereas in Latin America there have been a number of shifts in competitiveness, but on a lower scale than those recorded by some developing countries during the previous two years.

E. Private capital flows to emerging markets

Net private capital flows to developing and transition economies increased in 1999, but at most only marginally from the levels recorded in 1998, which themselves represented a fall of more than 50 per cent from those of 1997 and reflected the aftermath of the financial crises in East Asia and the Russian Federation. This outcome was accompanied by a more stable environment for major financial indicators than that of the preceding two years. For the year 2000 forecasts range from at most limited change to a significant increase in flows, but one which would still leave private financing well short of its previous peak. Such forecasts are nonetheless tentative: those responsible for them emphasize especially their dependence on the avoidance of a return of turbulence to global financial markets.

1. Developments in 1999

The two sets of estimates in table 3.8 both show a small increase in net private capital flows to developing and transition economies from 1998 to 1999.[18] These estimates for 1999 display regional divergences. Recovery was recorded for inflows into Asia, whilst in Latin America the inflow was substantially reduced. By contrast, the changes for economies in both Europe and Africa were much more limited. There was also significant variation in the volatility of different categories of inflow: as in other recent years, estimates of FDI mostly showed either little change or rises in 1999, whilst those of debt securities and bank-lending were subject to greater variation.

The more limited impact of recent financial crises on FDI than on other major categories of private financial flow to developing and transition economies has been widely remarked upon. Once determined primarily by relatively long-term economic prospects and structural factors, FDI in recent years has come to be significantly influenced by privatization (which can have lumpy effects on a particular year's figures) and by the growing importance of cross-border merger and acquisition transactions (and thus by conditions in, and regulations regarding access to, national equity markets).[19] The rise in FDI in 1999 was associated with substantial receipts from privatization in Latin America (the especially large increase for Argentina, reflecting the sale of the petroleum conglomerate YPF to a Spanish company) and with asset sales in East Asia associated with bank and non-bank corporate restructuring and facilitated by the recent relaxation of restrictions on foreign investment.

Net private capital inflows in the form of debt declined sharply in 1999. The exposure of BIS-reporting banks in 1999 was 7 per cent lower than a year earlier, the decline affecting all regions containing major borrowers (see table 3.9). Well over 50 per cent of the total decline was due to the change in exposure to East and South Asian countries, though the absolute amount of this change for the region was considerably less than 1998. The severe contraction in 1998 reflected the widespread withdrawal of lending facilities to countries in the region in the aftermath of its financial crisis, including for a while those linked to the financing of trade flows. The 1999 contraction was influenced by continuing repayments of existing debt by some countries, but also in Asia by a reduced need for borrowing due to the accumulation of foreign-exchange reserves resulting from trade surpluses. Net outflows from the Russian Federation more than accounted for the decline in exposure to Eastern Europe, and much of the net outflow from Latin America was accounted for by Brazil, which nonetheless began to borrow substantial amounts late in the year. The declines in exposure have been accompanied by a widespread lengthening of maturities: in East and South Asia, for example, for the majority of countries with large borrowings from banks the proportion of their exposure with a residual ma-

Table 3.8

NET CAPITAL FLOWS TO DEVELOPING AND TRANSITION ECONOMIES, 1997–2000:
ESTIMATES BY IMF AND THE INSTITUTE FOR INTERNATIONAL FINANCE

(Billions of dollars)

Type of flow/region	1997	1998	1999	2000[a]
	Estimates of the Institute for International Finance			
Net private capital inflows				
Total	266	137	151	199
Private creditors	125	5	-12	26
Commercial banks	36	-59	-41	-11
Non-bank private creditors	89	63	29	37
Equity investment	142	133	162	172
Direct equity	116	119	141	130
Portfolio equity	26	14	21	42
Africa/Middle East	15	8	10	12
Asia/Pacific	67	4	40	59
Europe	76	37	34	35
Latin America	108	88	67	92
	Estimates of the International Monetary Fund			
Net private capital inflows[b]				
Total	148	75	81	71
Net direct investment	139	143	150	153
Net portfolio investment	53	9	23	30
Other net investment	-44	-77	-93	-113
Africa	17	12	15	16
Net direct investment	7	5	10	9
Net portfolio investment	4	4	4	3
Other net investment	6	2	1	4
Asia	-1	-43	-27	-30
Net direct investment	55	58	50	53
Net portfolio investment	4	-18	-5	6
Other net investment	-60	-83	-71	-90
Middle East and Europe	24	22	27	0
Net direct investment	3	3	3	9
Net portfolio investment	5	0	10	0
Other net investment	16	19	14	-9
Western hemisphere	86	70	54	70
Net direct investment	53	56	64	57
Net portfolio investment	19	15	11	13
Other net investment	13	-1	-20	0
Transition economies	23	14	12	15
New direct investment	20	21	24	25
Net portfolio investment	22	7	4	9
Other net investment	-18	-14	-16	-19

Source: Institute for International Finance, *Capital Flows to Emerging Market Economies,* 13 April 2000; IMF, *World Economic Outlook,* May 2000, table 2.2.

a Forecast.

b Other net investment comprises trade credits, loans, currency and deposits, and other assets and liabilities.

Table 3.9

EXTERNAL ASSETS OF BANKS IN THE BIS REPORTING[a] AREA VIS-À-VIS DEVELOPING AND TRANSITION ECONOMIES, 1997–1999

	1997	1998	1999	Stock in 1999
	(Percentage increase[b])			($ billion)
Total[c]	8.6	-7.7	-6.7	887
of which in:				
Latin America	11.3	-2.8	-5.5	280
Africa	19.6	0.3	8.1	45
West Asia	19.8	23.5	3.0	137
East and South Asia	1.1	-21.7	-14.5	315
Central Asia	35.5	17.6	26.7	3
Eastern Europe	19.4	-0.4	-4.6	96
Other Europe[d]	28.7	12.1	10.6	11
All borrowers[e]	15.4	3.0	2.6	9824

Source: BIS, *International Banking and Financial Market Developments*, various issues.

  a Including certain offshore branches of United States banks.
  b Based on data for end-December after adjustment for movements of exchange rates.
  c Excluding offshore banking centres, i.e. in Latin America: Bahamas, Barbados, Bermuda, Cayman Islands, Netherlands Antilles and Panama; in Africa: Liberia; in West Asia: Bahrain and Lebanon; and in East Asia: Hong Kong (China), Singapore and Vanuatu.
  d Malta, Bosnia and Herzegovina, Croatia, Slovenia, The former Yugoslav Republic of Macedonia, and Yugoslavia.
  e Including multilateral institutions.

turity of less than one year was at least 60 per cent at the end of 1997, but by the end of 1999 it had fallen to 50 per cent or less, except in the Republic of Korea and Taiwan Province of China.[20] During the same period there were (mostly smaller) movements in the same direction in the maturity structure of BIS-reporting banks' exposure to countries with large borrowing in Latin America and Eastern Europe.

Net issues of international debt instruments (money-market instruments and bonds) by developing and transition economies fell slightly in 1999 (table 3.10). Once again issues were heavily concentrated among Latin American borrowers, and among governments and state agencies. Much of new bond issuance in 1999 took place in the second quarter; this bunching reflected partly the bringing to the markets of bonds whose issuance had been postponed during the turbulence in international financial markets at the time of the Brazilian crisis. During the remainder of 1999 net issues continued at lower levels, but issuance accelerated in the first quarter of 2000. Gross issues by Latin American borrowers continued at much

higher levels than net issues owing to substantial refinancing throughout the year. Elsewhere net issuance in 1999 was low: in East and South Asia the figure was depressed by substantial repayments; and for Eastern European countries the fall from 1998 to 1999 reflected the exclusion from the international securities markets of the Russian Federation, which had been a large borrower in the first half of 1998. The yield spreads in secondary markets on the bonds of borrowers from emerging markets began the year 1999 at levels still reflecting the aftermath of the turbulence which followed the preceding summer (see chart 3.4). For most of these economies the rest of the year was marked by a fall in such spreads (which for most non-Latin American borrowers represented a continuation of trends already begun in the autumn of 1998), but this movement tended to peter out in the first quarter of 2000.

Estimates of the Institute for International Finance (IIF) indicate a rise of net cross-border flows of equity investment into developing and transition economies, though to a level still below that of 1997.[21] This rise was accompanied by

Table 3.10

INTERNATIONAL ISSUANCE OF DEBT SECURITIES[a] BY DEVELOPING AND TRANSITION ECONOMIES, 1997–2000

(Billions of dollars)

	Gross issues				Net issues			
	1997	*1998*	*1999*	*2000 (First quarter)*	*1997*	*1998*	*1999*	*2000 (First quarter)*
Total	148.0	89.5	79.7	33.0	82.1	36.3	33.6	20.5
of which in:								
Latin America	75.5	43.4	48.0	17.6	41.1	22.5	26.4	13.7
East and South Asia	49.3	11.7	16.3	7.8	25.4	-0.7	-1.1	4.3
Eastern Europe	11.7	21.3	5.2	2.3	9.0	14.6	1.6	0.0
Memo item:								
World	1508.6	1657.2	2305.0	688.1	560.4	681.5	1225.2	266.0

Source: UNCTAD secretariat calculations, based on BIS, *International Banking and Financial Market Developments*, various issues.
  a International money market instruments and international bonds and notes, classified by residence of issuer.

a boom in equity prices in these markets (of more than 80 per cent in dollar terms in East and South Asia and of more than 50 per cent in Latin America).[22] Most of these equity flows involved shares issued in the stock markets of the recipient countries, but part also consisted of new shares issued in external markets in the form of primary and secondary placements. The latter rose from about $9 billion in 1998 to more than $20 billion in 1999, a rise which reflected mainly an increase by issuers from East and South Asia, from about $5 billion to almost $17 billion.[23]

2. Outlook

There is considerable uncertainty regarding the outlook for private capital flows to developing and transition economies in 2000. This uncertainty is reflected in differences in the direction of change forecast for such flows by major institutions. Thus, as shown in table 3.8, IIF forecasts a rise in net inflows over 1999 but still to a level only 75 per cent of that attained in 1997, while IMF (using a larger sample of countries) forecasts some small contraction.[24] The rise forecast by IIF is largely due to a turnaround of about $40 billion in net debt inflows, whilst the con-

traction forecast by IMF is strongly influenced by the change in net flows of non-securitized debt (after deduction of outflow on the part of residents which are not allowed for in the IIF figures). The IIF's expectation of a turnaround reflects a forecast increase in issuance of international bonds and a continuing reduction in the contraction of net bank-lending, associated, *inter alia*, with a decrease in repayments, particularly by some Asian borrowers.[25] Both institutions forecast rises in net equity flows for 2000, though for IIF the increase reflects a fall in FDI which is more than counterbalanced by an increase in net portfolio equity flows.[26]

Forecasts for 2000 are qualified by those responsible by references to elements of considerable uncertainty in the present outlook. Some of the uncertainty is associated with recent volatility in major equity markets and with the effects of a probable tightening of monetary policy in major industrialized countries. The periods of turbulence of 1997–1998 serve as a reminder that the channels of global transmission of the effects of shifts in exchange rates and asset prices are not yet fully understood, and thus increase the hazardousness of financial forecasts. Such effects, through their impact on investors' preferences and perceptions of creditworthiness, may manifest

Chart 3.4

YIELD SPREAD OF SELECTED INTERNATIONALLY ISSUED EMERGING-MARKETS BONDS,[a] JANUARY 1998 TO APRIL 2000

(Basis points[b])

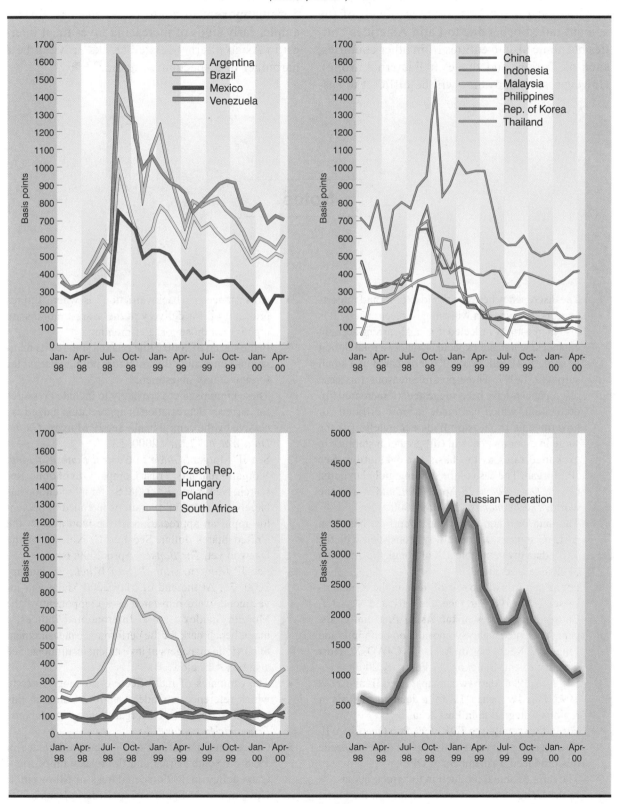

Source: Primark Datastream.

  a Differential between the yield of a representative bond issued by the borrowing country and that of the same maturity issued by the government of the country in whose currency the borrower's bonds are denominated.

  b One basis point equals 0.01 per cent.

themselves in any or all of the major categories of private capital flows to developing and transition economies. Other uncertainties involve particular categories of flows. For example, new announced bond issues in the first quarter of 2000 exceeded $25 billion, which is more than 40 per cent of that for 1999 as a whole (much of the amount raised being due to Latin American entities but some also to entities from other countries, such as Turkey and those of Eastern Europe). However, such buoyancy will be difficult to sus-

tain as rates of interest increase for major currencies. Other unpredictable elements involve portfolio equity flows. During the early months of 2000 there was some pulling back by international investors in portfolio equities from emerging markets, particularly in respect of East and South Asia. Yet this movement could be reversed if, for example, early signs of increasing investment interest in Asian internet-related stocks prove to be a harbinger of a speculative boom.[27] ■

Notes

1 The discrepancy between world exports and imports appears to have been widening in recent years. It is also increasingly reflected in global current-account balances, which are expected to show a total deficit of some $245 billion in 2000, compared to a small surplus in 1997. Three possible reasons for these discrepancies have been suggested: (i) increased liberalization, which has made it more difficult for governments to measure trade accurately; (ii) the surge in e-commerce; and (iii) greater instability in exchange rates as the basis for evaluation. See JP Morgan, The case of the missing global exports, *Global Data Watch*, 28 April 2000; and War of the world, *The Economist*, 27 May 2000.

2 The data on Latin American countries, based on ECLAC sources, are not always consistent with the WTO data given in table 3.1, although the direction of change is identical.

3 For an analysis of the role of trade in the Asian crisis see *TDR 1998*, Part One, chap. III; and Akyüz Y, Causes and sources of the Asian financial crisis, paper presented to the Symposium on Economic and Financial Recovery in Asia, UNCTAD X, Host Country Event, Bangkok, 17 February 2000.

4 See *TDR 1996*, Part Two, chaps. I and II, and *TDR 1993*, Part Two, chap. IV, for a detailed analysis of regional integration in East Asia.

5 For further details, see *TDR 1999*, Part One, chap. II.

6 The average spot price of the basket of seven crude oils produced by members of OPEC.

7 The ratio of actual production to agreed quotas.

8 In the United States, every $1 change in the barrel price of oil translates into a 1 per cent change in the consumer price index (CPI) for energy. Energy has a weight of about 6.3 per cent; hence, the estimated 0.3 per cent for a price rise of $5.2.

9 An instance of "backwardation" is where futures prices of oil for delivery in the nearest months are higher than those for later months.

10 In the spring of 2000 Chile relaxed some of its regulations concerning the minimum holding period for foreign equity investment.

11 These circumstances are likely to include pressures for currency depreciation or appreciation judged excessive by the central bank. See JP Morgan, *Global Data Watch,* 12 May 2000: 53.

12 See JP Morgan, *Guide to Central Bank Watching*, Morgan Guaranty Trust Company Economic Research, New York, 2000: 38. So far intervention has largely consisted of operations intended to prevent too rapid an appreciation of the won against the United States dollar. See Lee C, Not out of the Daewoo yet, *The Banker*, April 2000: 63.

13 See JP Morgan, *Global Data Watch*, 28 January 2000: 75. At the end of May 2000 Malaysian investments were reinstated as a component of the Morgan Stanley Capital International Indices, a major benchmark for the performance measurement of portfolio managers of investment institutions. See also box 4.1 below.

14 The estimates of real effective exchange rates to which reference is made at various points in this section are those in JP Morgan, *Emerging Markets: Economic Indicators*.

15 Concerning the effects of financial turbulence in 1998 on South Africa and the relaxation of monetary policy in 1999, see address of Mboweni T, Governor, at the South African Reserve Bank's 79th ordinary general meeting, 24 August 1999 (reprinted in *BIS Review*, 31 August 1999).

16 Net FDI on an annualized basis during the same period amounted to 3.5 per cent of GDP. In 1999

net foreign portfolio investment in annualized dollar terms varied from minus $0.8 billion in the first half of the year to a positive $2.9 billion in the second half. See JP Morgan, *Global Data Watch*, 4 February 2000 (p. 47), 3 March 2000 (p. 16), and 5 May 2000 (p. 11).

17 *TDR 1999,* Part One, chap. III, sect. C.2.

18 Figures of some other institutions, estimated on different bases, actually show declines during this period. For example, estimates of JP Morgan show net private capital flows to developing and transition economies declining from $182 billion in 1998 to $153 billion in 1999 (JP Morgan, *World Financial Markets,* 14 April 2000: 34). Those of the World Bank show a decline from $268 billion to $239 billion (World Bank, *Global Development Finance 2000*, Washington, DC, World Bank, 2000, table 2.1). Such differences, especially in the estimated size of the flows, reflect partly different coverage and methods of estimation. Thus, the estimates of IIF are before substraction of net lending by residents and changes in monetary gold and errors and omissions in the balance of payments (which typically represent a substantial proportion of its figures for net private flows) and comprise a sample of 29 "emerging-market economies". Those of IMF are on a balance-of-payments basis and are thus net of outflows by residents. Moreover, they cover the great majority of IMF member countries. The World Bank's estimates also cover a large number of countries, but are limited to long-term transactions and do not include outflows by residents. The figures of JP Morgan can be assumed to be estimated on a basis closer to that of IIF than of IMF.

19 Cross-border merger and acquisition transactions involving sales by developing economies (a substantial part of which are financed by FDI) tended to accelerate in the 1990s. See *TDR 1999,* chap. V; and *World Investment Report 1999,* United Nations publication, sales no. E.99.II.D.3, New York and Geneva, 1999, annex tables B.1 and B.7.

20 The exposure of BIS-reporting banks to the Republic of Korea with a residual maturity of one year or less fell from levels well over 60 per cent in 1997 to as low as 45 per cent in 1998, but subsequently rose to 58 per cent at the end of 1999, an increase due more to reductions in the residual maturity of loans initially made at longer maturities than to short-term borrowing. See Basel Committee on Banking Supervision, Supervisory lessons to be drawn from the Asian crisis, *Basel Committee on Banking Supervision Working Paper No. 2,* Bale, BIS, June 1999, tables 2 and 5, and BIS press release of 11 May 2000 ("BIS consolidated international banking statistics for end-December 1999"). The statistics used here are based on a BIS-reporting system different from that used for table 3.9.

21 The 1999 figure was depressed by the technical factors associated with estimation of the balance-of-payments impact on Argentina of the sale referred to above of the oil company YPF to a Spanish company, which resulted in negative flows of portfolio equity investment reflecting continuing minority holdings by residents of Argentina. See IIF, *Capital Flows to Emerging Market Economies,* 13 April 2000: 9.

22 IIF, *Capital Flows to Emerging Market Economies,* 24 January 2000: 8–9.

23 BIS, *International Banking and Financial Market Developments,* June 2000, table 17.

24 Like IIF, JP Morgan also forecasts a rise in net private capital flows to "emerging economies", from $153 billion in 1999 to $179 billion in 2000. See JP Morgan, *World Financial Markets,* 14 April 2000: 34.

25 Substantial repayments are forecast, nevertheless, for Indonesia and Thailand. See IIF, *Capital Flows to Emerging Market Economies,* 13 April 2000: 5.

26 Most of the decline forecast by IIF is due to Argentina, whose total for 1998 was boosted by the sale of YPF referred to earlier (see note 21 above). JP Morgan forecasts a small contraction in net equity flows to "emerging economies", reflecting declines in both portfolio and direct investment. See JP Morgan, *World Financial Markets,* 14 April 2000: 34.

27 An example of the spreading to East Asia of speculative investment interest in this sector of a kind more familiar in certain major industrialized countries is provided by a Malaysian conglomerate with interests in construction and telecommunications. Reversing a decision to sell its telecommunications subsidiaries as part of efforts to reduce its debt in January 2000, the company instead changed its name to one including dotcom. In a matter of weeks its stock price increased by more than 150 per cent. See Hamlin K, Is corporate Asia getting the message?, *Institutional Investor (International Edition)*, March 2000.

Chapter IV

CRISIS AND RECOVERY IN EAST ASIA

A. Introduction

The speed of recovery in East Asian emerging markets most affected by the financial crisis has astounded the most optimistic observers, even though a Mexican-style V-shaped recovery was widely predicted for most economies in the region. Even institutions such as IMF, which have had first-hand information on the state of the economies concerned and exerted a major influence on the policies pursued in response to the crisis, now see their original projections of economic growth in the region exceeded by a large margin. The Republic of Korea is an outstanding case in point, where the growth rate came close to 11 per cent in 1999, compared to an IMF projection in May 1999 of 2 per cent. The economies of ASEAN-4 (Indonesia, Malaysia, Philippines and Thailand) also recovered, growing at an average of almost 3 per cent in 1999, as opposed to earlier IMF projections of a further contraction of activity. The speed of recovery in the region has also belied the forecasts of other institutions and observers, including the UNCTAD secretariat, which disagreed with the orthodox diagnosis and policy response to the crisis.[1]

There are conflicting claims regarding the origin and nature of this recovery. While, on one view, the speed of the recovery represents a vindication of the international policy approach to the crisis, on another it discredits the orthodox diagnosis that these economies suffered from serious structural and institutional shortcomings and that they would be unable to resume growth un-

less these shortcoming were effectively addressed. Quite apart from apportioning responsibilities and credits, an examination of the recovery process has its own merits in that not only it would help to better understand the causes of such crises but, and more fundamentally, it would also yield invaluable lessons for better management of similar crises when they occur.

The examination of the recovery process in this chapter lends support to a number of conclusions:

- The policy response in terms of monetary tightening aggravated the impact of the currency crisis on the financial and corporate sectors, and served to depress production and employment further without bringing stability. Currencies were stabilized not as a result of increases in interest rates, but of the build-up of reserves due to massive import cuts and the reduction in foreign claims resulting from debt rescheduling and also of the imposition of capital controls. Thus, in retrospect, provision of adequate international liquidity to replenish reserves, together with exchange controls, debt standstill and maturity rollover (i.e. the kind of measures advocated in *TDR 1998*), would have been a much more effective response than a policy of high interest rates.

- The speed of recovery owed a great deal to policies pursued after the initial tightening.

The strong response of the economies concerned to subsequent fiscal and monetary easing suggests that initial policies created an unnecessarily tight squeeze. The economies bounced back rapidly when the policy of austerity was reversed and governments were allowed to play a more positive role in recovery. This policy reversal was brought about by the deepening of the crisis and widespread criticisms, rather than constituting part of a carefully sequenced policy package.

- The speed of recovery was not due to the elimination of structural weaknesses that were given great weight in explaining the crisis. Indeed, despite their subsequent reversal, the raising of interest rates caused serious dislocations in the corporate and financial sectors, aggravating rather than eliminating structural weaknesses. Financial and corporate restructuring has only just started. This suggests that the recoveries are not firmly based and that the structural difficulties may reassert themselves, possibly leading to a W-shaped recovery.

- Although in most countries seriously affected by the crisis per capita incomes are now above or close to prior levels, income appears to be less equally distributed. In particular, employment and labour earnings have lagged behind aggregate income, and poverty has remained considerably above pre-crisis levels. On some accounts it could take East Asia a decade to eliminate the poverty created by the financial crisis. This is consistent with the general pattern observed in emerging markets that boom-bust-recovery cycles tend to be regressive in terms of income distribution and poverty, even when their overall impact on economic growth may be neutral.

- The crisis has longer-term implications for economic development of the region not only because it has led to structural dislocations in the corporate and financial sectors, but also, and above all, because it has laid bare the kind of vulnerability that the region is exposed to as a result of its excessive reliance on foreign markets and capital for economic growth. This may call for a reconsideration of development strategy.

B. The policy response to the crisis and the recovery process

There have been significant differences among the countries regarding both the causes and the evolution of the crisis, as well as the nature and the speed of recovery.[2] While all countries that were seriously affected generally had large short-term and other liquid international liabilities as a result of a surge in arbitrage inflows, their exposure to a rapid exit of foreign capital varied considerably; for instance, in contrast to other countries, in Malaysia short-term external debt was more than covered by international reserves. There were also differences in the use made of capital inflows. In some countries, notably the Republic of Korea, there was excessive manufacturing investment in relation to demand and output, generated by a drive for an export market

share at the expense of profitability, while in others, notably Thailand, there was a speculative surge in the property market, supported by capital inflows. Similarly, some private firms in South-East Asia had invested heavily in other non-traded activities, notably in physical infrastructure, with funds borrowed abroad. On the eve of the crisis, macroeconomic fundamentals regarding the external accounts were much less favourable in Thailand than elsewhere in the region. Indeed, the Thai crisis emerged as a typically balance-of-payments one, aggravated by excessive short-term debt and capital-account openness, while the other economies suffered primarily from contagion. The sudden loss of confidence in Thailand appears to have been greatly influenced by three major concerns: the current-account deficit, which had been rising constantly from 1993 onwards to reach 8 per cent of GDP in 1995–1996; the considerable volume of short-term and other liquid foreign liabilities, which exceeded liquid international assets by a large margin; and, to a lesser extent, an appreciated currency.

The balance-of-payments fundamentals were better in the other countries of the region, although many of them were financially vulnerable because of a rapid accumulation of short-term and other liquid foreign liabilities. In particular, in Indonesia there was little currency appreciation, and the current deficit as a proportion of GDP was less than half that of Thailand. At some 4 per cent of GDP, the current-account deficit of the Republic of Korea was not much above the levels of previous decades, and it was already falling. Malaysia had a greater appreciation and moderately larger current-account deficit. The balance-of-payments fundamentals of the Philippines were worse than in both the Republic of Korea and Indonesia, but its external financial vulnerability was much less. While all the currencies in the region came under attack, it was the extent of external financial vulnerability and speculative pressures that were the determining factors in the incidence of the crisis.

Indonesia fell into deeper recession than its neighbours and its recovery has also been weak and disorderly, despite its better initial macroeconomic fundamentals, primarily as a result of the political turmoil brought about by the effects of the crisis on living conditions and the dispute over the causes of the crisis and appropriate policy response, which also involved international agencies. The economic and social effects were particularly disruptive because incomes of a large segment of the population were generally not very much above the poverty threshold. In Thailand and the Republic of Korea policy responses were designed to maintain free movement of capital, using monetary and fiscal tightening to restore confidence. In the Republic of Korea there was a sharp decline of output, despite its more robust and resilient industrial structure and the absence of any significant speculative investment in property and non-performing loans linked to such financing, but recession was even deeper in Thailand. Malaysia's initial policy response was also orthodox, but it subsequently introduced capital controls in order to stabilize its currency and to gain autonomy for an expansionary monetary policy to grow out of the crisis. Compared to Thailand, the decline

in output in Malaysia was moderate, and its recovery has also been more robust.

A close examination of the evolution of policies and economic performance in the region reveals valuable lessons regarding the limits of orthodox macroeconomic policies under conditions of payments crisis originating in the capital account, as opposed to traditional payments crises associated with macroeconomic imbalances and difficulties in financing current-account deficits. As discussed in some detail in past issues of *TDR*, increases in interest rates failed to bring currency stability while deepening recession. This was also noted by the Government of the Republic of Korea in a report to the G-20, which referred to "malign side-effects" of high interest rates, including the "accelerated slowdown in real economic activity through the contraction of consumption and investment; the greatly increased incidence of corporate failures; and the further increase in non-performing loans of financial institutions".[3] Indeed, the financial difficulties brought about by sharp currency depreciations and interruption of external credit lines were aggravated by high interest rates, which made the carrying costs of debt unsustainable. With falling domestic sales and export revenues, firms found it impossible to meet their commitments to financial institutions which had already been weakened by the corporate bankruptcies (as in the Republic of Korea) or the collapse of the property market (as in Thailand).

Indeed, evidence suggests that currency depreciation inflicted much less damage on firms than the rise in interest rates and cut-backs in domestic credit lines because many firms with large foreign indebtedness were export-oriented:[4] if credit lines had been maintained, greater competitiveness and growing export revenues would have provided a cushion against rising liabilities in domestic currency as a result of depreciations. In this respect, firms in Asia were in a much better position than those in other emerging-market countries.[5]

While rising interest rates failed to stabilize currencies by restoring confidence, they did so indirectly by making a major contribution to a sharp fall in domestic demand, which, together with the lack of liquidity, produced a decline in industrial production, employment and consumption, leading to massive cuts in imports. In the Republic of Korea, for instance, imports fell from

Box 4.1

THE RATIONALE AND EFFECTS OF CAPITAL CONTROLS IN MALAYSIA

Although, like the Republic of Korea and Thailand, Malaysia experienced a surge in short-term capital inflows in the first half of the 1990s, on the eve of the outbreak of the crisis in 1997 the maturity structure of its external debt was much more favourable than in those two countries, and its reserves were more than enough to cover its short-term foreign liabilities, reaching some 70 billion ringgit, compared to liabilities of 36 billion ringgit (of which some 27 billion were owed by the banking sector). At the end of 1997 total external debt was only 40 per cent of GDP and the debt service ratio was below 7 per cent. Furthermore, although the banks carried a disproportionate share of private-sector financing, with loans amounting to 150 per cent of GDP, the reforms put in place after the mid-1980s had strengthened the financial sector: property loans carried collateral well over 100 per cent, while loans to finance equity positions were no more than 8 per cent of the total. In June 1997 the non-performing loan ratio was not much above 2 per cent, and the risk-weighted capital ratio of the banking system was around 12 per cent, well above the Basle ratio of 8 per cent, while the ratio of provisions to non-performing loans was nearly 100 per cent. On the fiscal side, 1997 was the fifth year of surplus, at more than 2 per cent of GDP.[1]

Despite these relatively favourable financial conditions, the pressures on the Malaysian currency were similar to those in other crisis-stricken countries. The exchange rate collapsed from 2.6 ringgit to the dollar in July 1997 to 4.7 in January 1998, the Kuala Lumpur equity index fell from around 1000 to 300 at its low, and non-performing loans in the banking sector reached over 12 per cent. Clearly, excessive short-term debt was not the main reason. Indeed, even after the crisis broke out there was no substantial capital outflow, such as occurred in the Republic of Korea and Thailand, and reserves never fell below 50 billion ringgit. The main reason was the speculation against the ringgit, facilitated by the existence of an offshore market in Singapore.

As in the other two countries, the initial response to the collapse of the currency and the increase in inflation was a tightening of monetary policy against a background of continued fiscal discipline. As a result, in the first nine months of 1998, GDP was 6 per cent below the corresponding period of the previous year, leading to sharp cuts in imports and a rapid turnaround in the current balance of payments, which reached a surplus of over 12 per cent of GDP. However, unlike the Republic of Korea or Thailand, since Malaysia never suffered from a lack of collateral to meet its short-term foreign commitments, the improved payments situation did not have the same stabilizing effect on its exchange rate. As a result of the impact of the weaknesses in the corporate sector on bad loans, new bank lending fell to almost zero as banks tried to shore up their balance sheets.

In the face of the sharp decline in output, a decision was taken to support the economy through fiscal stimulus and monetary expansion so as to ease the liquidity crunch. But given the weak economic conditions and continued speculative pressures, much of the increased liquidity leaked abroad. To prevent this liquidity drain, a $2 million limit was placed in August 1997 on Malaysian banks' currency swaps with non-residents in transactions unrelated to trade. However, the result was to shift borrowing to the Singapore offshore market. At the beginning of 1998 offshore ringgit deposit rates rose to over 20 per cent, and eventually reached 40 per cent, compared with domestic rates of around 11 per cent. The only plausible justification for such a differential was speculation against the ringgit. The existence of the offshore market thus not only undermined the efforts by the Central Bank to reduce interest rates and expand liquidity in order to support economic activity, but also impeded the stabilization of the currency. The decision was thus taken to close the Singapore market by making offshore ringgit transactions illegal. This market had played a role similar to that of the offshore banking market in the Bangkok International Bank Facility, but unlike the latter, which had been created by conscious steps, it was an historical artifact.[2] Since it could not be directly regulated or controlled by Malaysia, the only alternative was to bring it onshore, which is what the regulations did.

In a series of measures introduced at the beginning of September 1998, domestic banks were prohibited from lending to non-resident banks and stockbrokers, or from engaging in any swap or repurchase transactions with non-residents, to eliminate non-resident ownership of ringgit balances held abroad. In addition, transactions in external ringgit accounts could only be made for the sale and purchase of ringgit assets, and balances could not be transferred among non-residents. Finally, since one of the major reasons for holding offshore balances was to hedge commercial transactions denominated in ringgit, domestic residents were required to invoice all external transactions in foreign currency, and the import and export of ringgit notes was strictly limited. As a result, it became impossible to settle ringgit contracts except through Malaysian banks in Malaysia.[3]

These measures designed to insulate domestic interest rates from external rates were combined with a decision to peg the exchange rate, a decision that was greatly influenced by the resumption of the decline of the currency with the onset of the Russian crisis.[4] Indeed, from July 1998 onwards the currency showed a tendency to return to post-crisis lows, even though the measures taken were bearing fruit in improving macroeconomic conditions regarding the fiscal balance, the payments surplus and inflation. Although the fixing of the exchange rate at 3.8 ringgit to the dollar represented a substantial appreciation from the then prevailing market rate, it was consistent with underlying macroeconomic conditions: the foreign account was already well in surplus and threatened to create an excessively strong expansion, foreign reserves were around four months' imports and double the level of short-term foreign claims.

Measures to control capital flows were selective: long-term flows and FDI were not regulated, and the currency continued to be fully convertible for commercial transactions as long as they were undertaken through Malaysian banks. In assessing these measures[5] it is important to recall that they were not introduced in an emergency to control excessive capital outflows, nor were they introduced to support unsustainable macroeconomic policies and conditions, such as rising fiscal and payments deficits and inflation. They were introduced well over a year after the outbreak of the crisis, during which time most of the foreign short-term capital had already left, domestic adjustment had already taken place, the balance of payments had moved into a large surplus, inflation had stabilized, and steps had already been taken to strengthen the financial and corporate sectors. Finally, it was made clear that the controls were temporary, and would be removed so as to allow non-resident holders to exit the ringgit once external conditions had stabilized. In fact, the rapid recovery of the economy allowed the progressive removal of the controls from February 1999.

Thus, those factors which had brought exchange stability and allowed interest rates to be reduced in the Republic of Korea and Thailand were not operating in Malaysia because of the interest rate differentials between onshore and offshore ringgit markets. Consequently, improved macroeconomic fundamentals did not work through greater exchange market stability. The success of the measures taken was confirmed by the fact that when the controls were lifted in September 1999 there was an immediate outflow of only 5.2 billion ringgit, and another 3.1 billion in the rest of the year. In the first quarter of 2000 there was a net inflow of 8.5 billion ringgit, an amount roughly equal to what had flown out at the expiry of the controls.[6] By May 2000 total official reserve assets were $32 billion, over six times short-term debt.[7] In December 1999 Malaysia's long-term foreign currency rating was raised to BBB and more recently the country was returned to the Morgan Stanley Capital International emerging market securities benchmark indices, indicating a normalization of relations with international capital markets.

---

[1]   See Bank Negara Malaysia, *Annual Report 1998*, Kuala Lumpur, 1999: 31-33.

[2]   Ibid.: 69–71.

[3]   For a full account of these measures see Bank Negara Malaysia, op. cit.: 214–219; the amendments introduced in February 1999 are documented in the Bank's *Annual Report 1999*, Kuala Lumpur, 2000.

[4]   For an alternative account that suggests exchange markets in the region had already stabilized when the measures were taken see IMF, *World Economic Outlook*, Oct. 1999, box 2.4.

[5]   See, for example, the assessment by Bank Negara Malaysia in its *Annual Report 1998*: 61 *et seq*.

[6]   Bank Negara Malaysia, *Economic and Financial Developments in the Malaysian Economy in the First Quarter of 2000* (www.bnm.gov.my/pub/info/index.htm).

[7]   See Bank Negara Malaysia, Press Release of 30 May 2000, Detailed disclosure of international reserves as at end April 2000 (www.bnm.gov.my/pa/2000/0530b.htm).

$142 billion in 1997 to $90 billion in 1998; together with a modest expansion in exports, the effect was a rapid reversal in the current balance, from a deficit of $8 billion to a surplus of $41 billion, or a staggering 14 per cent of GDP. The rapid increase in reserves, along with a rescheduling of more than 95 per cent of commercial banks' short-term debt, restored confidence in the currency and finally brought stability to the foreign-exchange market. Simultaneously, the expansionary impact of the current-account surplus on the liquidity of the economy allowed interest rates to be reduced; by the third quarter of 1998 they had returned to their pre-crisis levels.

Thus, it was the sharp recovery in foreign exchange reserves due to the improved current payments situation produced by a slump in imports, together with the declines in foreign claims due to rescheduling of short-term debt, that brought currency stability and the reversal of the tight interest rate policy. While rising interest rates failed to convince investors to hold domestic assets by enhancing their return, the collateral effect of the rise in usable reserves relative to foreign claims reassured foreign holders and stabilized the exchange rate.[6]

In Malaysia, too, the initial response in terms of higher interest rates failed to restore confidence and stabilize the currency while deepening the crisis. In view of continued speculation on the currency, the Government introduced temporary capital controls in September 1998, which turned out to be highly successful in stabilizing the currency and allowing the economy to recover (box 4.1).

In a sense, orthodox policies succeeded in stabilizing exchange rates not by restoring confidence through high interest rates, as intended, but by creating a deep recession. The experience thus suggests that "malign side-effects" of high interest rates could have been avoided by introducing a temporary debt standstill and bringing borrowers and lenders together to reschedule short-term debt, reinforced by a rapid provision of international liquidity to replenish reserves and provide current-account financing, rather than by trying to persuade investors to stay put by means of hikes in interest rates and the provision of funding to bail out creditors while keeping the capital account open.

An additional factor in bringing about exchange-rate stability was the policies adopted by China and Malaysia. Despite the adverse impact on its competitiveness of sharp currency depreciation in many countries in the region, China resisted the temptation of competitive devaluation. Similarly, the Malaysian success in tying its exchange rate to the dollar provided a stable anchor for the region, particularly in view of the importance of intraregional trade and of the stability of the regional pattern of exchange rates. From September 1998 onwards, the won, the rupiah and the baht all first showed stability and then registered moderate gains against the dollar. The Malaysian experience also demonstrates that fixing the nominal value of the currency does not necessarily lead to appreciation, provided that such a policy is accompanied by effective control over capital flows.

However, currency stability was not sufficient to bring about a turnaround in economic activity. Recovery occurred only when initial policies had been reversed and fiscal deficits and lower interest rates were allowed to operate to offset the massive reduction in domestic private spending. For instance, in the Republic of Korea, the first agreement reached with IMF, in December 1997, insisted on tight fiscal policy, but subsequent agreements recognized the inevitability of a fiscal deficit, setting it at some 0.8 per cent of GDP in February 1998, at 1.7 per cent in May of the same year, and eventually at around 5 per cent from July 1998 onwards.[7] By the second half of the year, the economy witnessed an unprecedented fiscal stimulus, together with interest rates that were nearly half of their pre-crisis levels. Fiscal expansion and growing exports brought about by lower interest rates, liquidity expansion and competitive exchange rates both stimulated demand and reduced constraints on supply, thereby pulling the economy out of recession and giving a strong push forward. Clearly, much of the recovery was of a technical nature, because the decline had been too fast and had gone too far. The discretionary fiscal stance continued to be expansionary in 1999, but rapid growth provided a cyclical fiscal correction, and a second supplementary budget to support low and middle-income groups was introduced to deal with the regressive effects of the crisis.

The rescheduling of foreign debt and the reversal of tight monetary and fiscal policy was not an orderly process. It was pursued much more rapidly in the Republic of Korea than in Thailand and Indonesia; together with the structural factors and initial conditions mentioned above, this difference of pace goes a long way in explaining why the recession was less deep, and the recovery stronger, than in the latter two countries.[8] In Malaysia, public consumption expenditure grew by over 7 per cent in 1997, but dropped by the same rate in 1998, followed by a rise of over 20 per cent in 1999; the budget deficit rose from less than 2 per cent of GDP in 1998 to almost 6 per cent in 1999. However, what distinguished Malaysia from the other countries was its interest rate policy. From Spring 1998 onwards, the rates were kept relatively low; for instance, in May 1998 the interbank lending rate was 11 per cent, compared to some 19 per cent in the Republic of Korea, 21 per cent in Thailand and 46 per cent in Indonesia. These differences did not simply reflect differences in inflation rates, as inflation was not much lower than in the Republic of Korea or Thailand. However, as continued availability of domestic credit at low interest rates created opportunities for speculation against the ringgit, control over capital flows became essential for stabilizing the currency and initiating recovery (see box 4.1). After the introduction of capital controls, interest rates were reduced further throughout 1999, falling to some 3 per cent in December, compared to 5 per cent in Thailand, 6.7 per cent in the Republic of Korea, and 13 per cent in Indonesia. With hindsight, the competition and challenge posed by the alternative policy approach adopted in Malaysia to the orthodox model, and its success in stabilizing the currency and initiating recovery, appear to have played an important role in the reversal of orthodox policies in the region and in the adherence to more realistic monetary and fiscal policies.

However, the damage inflicted on corporations and the financial system by high interest rates was irreparable. As examined in some detail in *TDR 1998*, monetary tightening aggravated the debt deflation process already under way as a result of the massive capital outflow, leading to widespread bankruptcies. Furthermore, some of the measures introduced to strengthen the financial system in the midst of debt deflation in fact resulted in increased fragility. In the Republic of Korea, for instance, as firms scrambled to reduce their domestic and foreign indebtedness and banks sought to cover their non-performing loans, the Government imposed the BIS capital requirements on banks, making it virtually impossible for firms to obtain even export credits.[9] The resulting loss in income through the virtual cessation of business activity in early 1998 also aggravated the debt

deflation process by forcing firms to liquidate assets at fire-sale prices in order to overcome the liquidity constraint, in effect causing serious dislocations in corporate balance sheets. The squeeze on corporations was further aggravated by efforts to reduce leverage as high debt-equity ratios were seen as the root cause of the crisis.

In view of the inability of the banking system to provide liquidity, the financing for business had to come from sales revenues. This puts into perspective the crucial role played by the rise in exports and the relaxation of the fiscal stance in providing finance for the recovery. However, the recovery has been unable to restore the health of the banking system or corporate balance sheets, necessitating continued public intervention in the credit mechanism. In the Republic of Korea, for instance, the Government had to provide large loan guarantees for lending to small and medium-sized firms even in late 1999, when recovery was well under way.

Countries suffering from increased defaults and NPLs have adopted different strategies regarding intervention in the financial system and financial and corporate restructuring (box 4.2). In Thailand, where the authorities adopted a market-based approach towards bad loans in the private sector, restructuring has been slow. In Indonesia, the Republic of Korea and Malaysia a government-led approach has been adopted to bank restructuring: a large proportion of NPLs and of banks under distress have effectively been nationalized, and liquidity support or fresh capital has been provided by the public sector to many banks experiencing financial difficulties. This virtual nationalization has resulted in the Republic of Korea, for instance, in the Government now holding more than 50 per cent of the total shares in the largest surviving banks, three of which account for 25 per cent of total bank lending. Even those banks that appear sound have substantial exposure to subsidiaries (such as leasing companies), whose losses have yet to be recognized on fully consolidated balance sheets.

Thus, contrary to expectations, recovery has taken place without any major financial and corporate restructuring:

> ... historical experience suggests that the duration and speed of recovery from financial crises vary considerably from case to case, often depending on how effectively financial sector problems and corporate sec-

Box 4.2

ALTERNATIVE APPROACHES TO THE RESOLUTION OF BAD LOANS

The crisis in East Asia left many financial institutions insolvent. While non-bank financial intermediaries were allowed to fail in a number of countries (e.g. merchant banks in the Republic of Korea and finance companies in Thailand), most countries provided either direct or indirect support for the rescue of banks. Restoring solvency requires financial engineering on both the asset and the liability side of a bank's balance sheet. The losses created by revaluing the bad loans on the asset side must be covered by injecting new capital if the losses lead to a decline in bank capital below regulatory standards. Rescue operations differ in how these adjustments take place.

Recently there have been two major examples of large-scale bad-loan resolution: for thrift institutions in the United States and the banking sector in Japan. The United States experience was not immediately applicable to Asia because of the prior existence of a federally operated deposit insurance fund which had first claim on all bank assets. The primary activity of the regulators was to close the failed thrift institutions and try to realize the highest possible values for the assets underlying the bad loans as rapidly as possible. The task of the United States Resolution Trust Corporation (RTC) was primarily to close banks and realize assets rather than to try to save banks as going concerns through restructuring and recapitalization. In Japan various schemes were introduced to transfer bad loans from bank balance sheets to a government agency which was to attempt to recover the loans, but the initial approach was voluntary and the loans could be returned to banks if they could not be realized.[1]

In the aftermath of the crisis in East Asia, most countries removed bad loans from the balance sheets of the original bank lenders and transferred them to specialized agencies funded by governments, subject to a discount on the value of the loans. The agencies attempted either to collect the debt from the borrower or to take possession of the underlying assets in order to realize their value through sales in the market. As the majority of bank loans were initially extended on the basis of the evaluation of underlying collateral, the process was greatly facilitated. However, the absence of modern bankruptcy laws in many countries impeded the rapid transfer of ownership of the underlying collateral to creditors or the specialized agencies.

The Korean experience

In the Republic of Korea the powers of Korea Asset Management Corporation (KAMCO), created in 1962 as part of the Korea Development Bank, were extended in 1997 to deal with the non-performing loans (NPLs) of financial institutions and assets of distressed companies through the creation of a special fund. In 1999 the Corporation was further empowered to create joint venture asset management companies with the participation of private financial institutions. Its initial capital was provided from government funds.[2]

KAMCO has been highly innovative in approach, using asset-backed securities as well as more traditional means of sales and auctions in disposing of assets. It has also been highly profitable, realizing more from the sale of its acquired assets than it paid for them in the first place, partly because many companies were only facing liquidity problems and were not technically insolvent. Thus, the extremely rapid recovery of the economy brought recovery in the earning power of the assets acquired by KAMCO. In 1999 KAMCO sold NPLs that it had acquired for 4 billion won for over 5 billion won. It is estimated that it has earned an average return of 10 per cent on its portfolio. As a result, it was able to operate on the basis of its own earnings rather than seek additional public funds when it acquired $17 billion of Daewoo bad loans from investment companies.[3]

Thailand's market-based approach

The Thai approach has been closest to that of the United States. A Financial Sector Restructuring Authority (FRA) was created in 1997 in order to deal with the 16 finance companies that had been suspended before the crisis broke out in July, but its operations were extended subsequently to deal with some 90 institutions. It has no other responsibilities and has a limited life of three years to complete its task.[4] The Thai programme is usually described as more market-based than those in other countries because FRA only assesses the viability of the rehabilitation plans submitted by the suspended finance companies. Moreover, restructuring in the rest of the financial sector is taking place outside any formal structure such as FRA and under the informal guidance of the Government and the Bank of Thailand, involving mergers, acquisitions by foreign buyers and closures.

In operations carried out by FRA the Government provided protection to all creditors of the suspended institutions, but their recapitalization or operation by the Authority was never envisaged. The institutions submitting acceptable plans would remain under its surveillance until they were judged capable of being returned to private operation and normal supervision by the Bank of Thailand. For others a more active role was envisaged for FRA, involving the appointment of management committees comprising representatives of the Ministry of Finance, the Bank of Thailand and FRA to replace the existing company directors, with the aim of preserving and maximizing the value of the remaining assets on behalf of creditors. These committees had the power to liquidate assets through public auctions, open also to international bidders, or via a liquidator, but again no provision was made for an injection of public capital or takeover.[5] Of the 56 company plans, so far only two have been accepted, which left the assets of the rest to be disposed of. The favoured method of disposal has been through public auction of loan pools, with the Asset Management Corporation (AMC) acting as bidder of last resort to set a floor to prices; for example, in the auction closed on 10 November 1999 AMC was the winning bidder in four out of nine offered tranches.[6] The auctions have been only moderately successful, in part because of widespread opposition to the sale of domestic assets at knockdown prices, and in part because of uncertainties in the existing bankruptcy and foreclosure laws with respect to guaranteeing access to the security on the loans.

The Malaysian approach

Just as Malaysia opted for a different policy response to the crisis, it also took a different, more proactive approach to financial sector restructuring. Two separate agencies were created to deal with the problems of the banking system. *Danaharta* was created as an asset management company to purchase and manage the sale of banks' NPLs. Banks with more than 10 per cent of NPLs were required to sell all such loans, failing which they would have to write down the value of the loans and liquidate them. *Danaharta* was empowered to impose on the borrowers of the loans acquired operating conditions that ensured maximum value recovery. Since sales of NPLs have been affected at market values, they resulted in losses to banks.[7] *Danamodal* was created to deal with such losses via recapitalization of potentially viable institutions. The Government thus became the strategic shareholder in these institutions, which aided the policy of bank merger and concentration pursued in order to create stronger and larger institutions.[8]

The most innovative aspect of the approach was the recognition that the health of the banking system was directly dependent on the health of the corporate sector, and that difficulties had often been caused by the shortage of liquidity rather than insolvency of the borrower – a problem that can be solved by ensuring continued lending to viable companies. Thus, the Corporate Debt Restructuring Committee was created to provide a platform for borrowers and creditors to work out feasible debt restructuring schemes without having to resort to legal proceedings and precipitating insolvency, and to ensure that financing was provided to companies during the process of restructuring so that liquidity shortage was not automatically transformed into insolvency. The scheme also provides a method for avoiding the difficulties caused by a legal framework which was not initially designed for facilitating corporate restructuring. The process is restricted to companies with aggregate bank borrowing of over 50 million ringgit from more than one financial institution. A creditors' committee, representing at least 75 per cent of the total debt of all creditors, must be established, and the creditors must agree to a 60-day standstill to determine the conditions of the company and the possibility of preserving it as a viable business. Stakeholder approval is required for workout proposals for debt restructuring formulated by the process. If there is a failure to reach agreement, *Danaharta* stands ready to intervene by purchasing NPLs to facilitate a workout agreement.[9]

[1]   See *TDR 1993*, Part Two, chap. I, sect. B.2. Subsequently a more active approach, closer to the United States model, was adopted, but the process of restructuring has remained extremely slow; see *TDR 1999*, chap. I, sect. B.1(b).
[2]   For the history of KAMCO see "Company History" (www.kamco.or.kr/eng/overview/main1.htm).
[3]   See Lee BJ, *KAMCO Pushes Transparency and Speed in Selling Distressed Assets, Reaps 10 Percent* (www.kamco.or.kr/kam); and KAMCO, *Annual Report 2000*, Acquisition result, "NPL Acquisition" (www.kamco.or.kr/eng/report/main.2.htm).
[4]   For a history of FRA see "About FRA" (www.fra.or.th/home_index.html).
[5]   See section 30 of "Emergency Decree on Financial Sector Restructuring B.E. 2540" (www.fra.or.th/home_index.html).
[6]   See "Results of the commercial and other loan sales as of November 10, 1999" (www.fra.or.th/home_index.html).
[7]   See "An introduction to Danaharta" (www.danaharta.com.my/default.html) and Bank Negara Malaysia, *Annual Report 1998*, Bangkok, 1999: 228–229.
[8]   See Bank Negara Malaysia, *Annual Report 1998*: 230–231.
[9]   See Bank Negara Malaysia, "Introduction to CDRC" (www.bnm.gov.my/crdc/intro.htm) and "Terms of reference of CDRC" (www.bnm.gov.my/cdrc/terms.htm); and Bank Negara Malaysia, *Annual Report 1998*: 230–233.

Table 4.1

CHANGES IN MACROECONOMIC RATIOS OVER RECENT FINANCIAL CYCLES IN SELECTED EAST ASIAN COUNTRIES

(Percentage points)

Country	Boom 1990– 1996[a]	Bust 1997– 1998	Recovery 1999
Indonesia			
Savings	-1.3	-7.6	-0.8
Investment	3.0	-18.1	-1.0
Budget balance	3.0	-4.4	-4.5
Current-account balance	-2.3	8.0	-1.0
Malaysia			
Savings	6.9	5.9	-1.7
Investment	8.0	-14.8	1.6
Budget balance	4.2	-3.9	-3.9
Current-account balance	-2.6	17.3	-1.3
Republic of Korea			
Savings	-1.9	-0.7	0.7
Investment	4.8	-17.5	6.4
Budget balance	-0.1	-4.4	0.4
Current-account balance	-7.2	17.3	-6.4
Thailand			
Savings	7.5	5.9	-5.5
Investment	13.9	-16.4	1.0
Budget balance	4.6	-5.9	-2.0
Current-account balance	-7.4	20.9	-4.1

Source: World Bank, *Country at a Glance,* various issues (www.worldbank.org/data); ESCAP, *Economic and Social Survey of Asia and the Pacific 2000*, United Nations publication, sales no. E.00.II.F.19, New York, 2000, tables II.14 and II.17.

Note: The ratio of each variable to GDP in the last year of each phase is compared with that in the terminal year of the preceding phase.

a 1991–1996 for Malaysia and 1988–1996 for Thailand.

tor difficulties ... are dealt with. In the current crisis, too, how deftly the financial and corporate sector problems are managed will be important – not only for the strength of the initial pickup in activity, but also for the prospects for sustained recovery.[10]

Indeed, the present recovery is probably more fragile than it may appear. Exports are unlikely to continue at the recent pace to provide either the markets or the liquidity needed to expand production, since the initial surge had one-off elements associated with the sharp swings in exchange rates. In the Republic of Korea, for instance, the trade surplus has virtually disappeared as imports surged with recovery and outstripped growth in exports: during January–May 2000 exports were some 29 per cent, but imports 41 per cent, higher than a year earlier. In Thailand imports rose by 20 per cent in 1999, while exports rose by 9 per cent. On the other hand, despite the recovery in employment and wages in the Republic of Korea, private consumption is following, rather than leading, income growth, and the household savings ratio is expected to rise over the coming years.[11] Private investment in 1998 was 25 per cent lower than in 1996 and is unlikely to regain its past level in the near future; in terms of its share in GDP, gross domestic investment fell by more than 10 percentage points from 1996 to 1999. The same goes for other countries in the region: in both Thailand and Malaysia private consumption rose in 1999 much less than income after sharp declines in 1998, and the share of investment in GDP was around 15 percentage points lower than in 1996 in both countries (table 4.1). In Malaysia, however, there was a sharp rebound in private consumption in the first quarter of 2000, when it rose 14 per cent above the corresponding period of 1999. This was the sharpest increase since the end of 1993. Together with investment, private consumption has become the main factor driving recovery, with the GDP growth rate reaching almost 12 per cent more than in the same quarter of the previous year. Otherwise, recovery in the region appears to be dependent on the fiscal stimulus, at least for the time being. In Thailand, where fiscal deficits are currently 7 per cent of GDP, it has been argued by IMF that "fiscal stimulus has been helpful and, if necessary, should be maintained over the next few quarters through the temporary extension of social spending programs. As the recovery becomes self-sustaining, it will become necessary to begin the task of fiscal consolidation, which is essential to check the growth in public debt".[12] But since domestic public debt is rising rapidly – from less than 16 per cent of GDP in 1996, it is projected to reach 40 per cent at the end of the current year – it is important that a quick transition be attained to a recovery that is driven by private demand.

Not only the speed but also the sources of the current recovery in East Asia are quite different from what was expected on the basis of orthodox diagnosis and interpretation of the crisis. For instance, according to a baseline scenario designed by IMF, recovery in the four most affected countries was expected to be driven primarily by private investment, even though many countries in the region were known to have significant excess capacity, while the contribution of public consumption and the foreign balance to growth was projected to be negative.[13]

In assessing the sustainability of the current recovery, it is important to note that so far global conditions have generally been favourable. The strength of the United States economy has been an important factor in the expansion of exports from the region. On the other hand, unlike in 1997, the recent rise of the dollar did not create serious problems of competitiveness, since the dollar has remained weak vis-à-vis the yen. While the recent increases in United States interest rates put some downward pressure on the East Asian currencies, notably in Thailand and the Philippines, this itself should cause no concern. However, as noted above, external payments are moving towards deficits and maintaining imports will require adequate capital inflows. Similarly, the region is relying on foreign capital to restructure its banks and corporations. Therefore, rising foreign interest rates could pose a dilemma: attracting foreign capital would call for a reversal of the monetary stance and higher interest rates which, in turn, could stifle growth by blocking the transition to a recovery led by private domestic demand and aggravating the difficulties of the banking system.

C. Macroeconomic and labour market indicators over the financial cycle

Large swings in economic activity associated with financial boom-bust-recovery cycles have far-reaching consequences for longer-term growth and development. Surges in capital inflows often lead to a deviation of key macroeconomic aggregates such as savings, investment, fiscal and foreign balances, exchange rates, employment and wages from their longer-term, sustainable levels. Rapid exit of capital and financial crises, on the other hand, tend to lead to overshooting in the opposite direction. The recovery process which restores aggregate income to pre-crisis levels generally results in a different configuration of key macroeconomic variables from those prevailing before the outbreak of the crisis. In this sense, financial cycles in emerging markets appear to be quite distinct from traditional business cycles. First, they tend to result in large shifts in income distribution and poverty, which can only be corrected after many years of growth. Second, the boom-bust process has implications for longer-term accumulation and growth; in some cases the pace of accumulation is expected to be dampened, whereas in others it may accelerate to the extent that the surge in capital inflows supports unsustainable consumption booms.

The remainder of this chapter addresses these issues. In this section an attempt is made to examine the shifts in key macroeconomic aggregates, labour market variables and poverty indicators over the full financial cycle in order to identify broad trends. In this analysis a comparison is made with some earlier episodes of financial crisis in other parts of the developing world, including the Southern Cone crisis in Argentina and Chile in the early 1980s and the crises of the 1990s in Argentina, Mexico, Turkey and Venezuela.[14] It considers the full financial cycle, distinguishing the different periods: before the surge in capital inflows (the *base* period); the *peak* of the boom in capital flows and economic activity; the *crisis* phase, characterized by a rapid exit of capital and a collapse of the currency; and the *recovery* phase, when aggregate income is restored to pre-crisis levels. Although, the duration of each of these phases and the behaviour of key variables therein vary from country to country, there are a number of common features in the boom-bust-recovery cycles in emerging markets.

1. The boom

Typically, surges in capital flows are associated with the widening of the gap between domestic income and absorption, and with rising external deficits, which often result from the effects of capital inflows themselves.[15] The resource gap usually originates from rising private consumption or investment, but there are also cases where capital inflows serve to finance large and sustained public-sector deficits.

The surge in capital inflows into East Asia started in the early 1990s, in some cases (such as the Republic of Korea) constituting a reversal of the previous capital outflow. By 1996, net annual inflows into the four countries most affected by the crisis had reached some $90 billion. The earlier episodes of surges in capital flows to emerging markets depict a similar picture. In most cases there was a substantial reversal from a net outflow to a net inflow, while in some there was a sharp increase in capital inflows within a short period, usually a single year. Such reversals occurred in Argentina in 1979 and 1991, and in Venezuela in the early 1990s. Chile experienced a fourfold increase in capital inflows in 1978, Mexico a sixfold one in 1990, and Turkey an 18-fold increase in 1990. Such booms lasted from three to seven years, and all ended up with rapid capital flight and financial crisis.[16]

In East Asia the surge in capital inflows was associated with a boom in private investment. In comparison to the base year, investment/GDP ratios in the peak of the financial cycle in Indonesia, Malaysia, Republic of Korea and Thailand were higher by 3–14 percentage points (table 4.1), exceeding 40 per cent in the last two countries. The increase was already from a very high base; investment ratios in the late 1980s were above 30 per cent of GDP. In Malaysia and Thailand, where savings ratios rose by some 7 percentage points during the boom phase in the early 1990s, the increase in investment ratios exceeded the rise in capital inflows as a percentage of GDP. In Indonesia and the Republic of Korea, on the other hand, the surge in capital inflows was not associated with any significant change in domestic savings ratios, with the rise in public-sector

surpluses compensating for a small decline in private savings.

By contrast, in the earlier Latin American episodes, surges in capital inflows were invariably associated with a boom in private consumption. Domestic savings ratios declined in all the booms, both during the late 1970s in the Southern Cone and during the first half of the 1990s in Argentina, Mexico and Venezuela (table 4.2). This inverse relationship between external and domestic savings has also been noted by ECLAC: "There is ... a considerable degree of substitution between domestic and external savings, particularly when financial flows are volatile, and ... variations in external savings are reflected, to a large extent, in increased or reduced public or private consumption."[17] The Turkish boom during 1989–1993, which in some respects resembled the Latin American pattern, was associated with a sharp rise in public spending, resulting in a 3.4 percentage points increase in the public-sector deficit as a proportion of GDP.

In all the four countries in East Asia, the boom was associated with a rapid increase in real wages, but in general labour productivity rose even faster (tables 4.3 and 4.4). In Malaysia and Thailand, real wage earnings in manufacturing rose moderately, on average by less than 5 per cent per annum. In the Republic of Korea the rise was much greater (7.6 per cent per annum during 1989–1996), but productivity growth was twice as fast. The gap between real wages and productivity growth provided some cushion against falling profitability of exports after the mid-1990s. Nevertheless, wages still recorded a sharp increase in dollar terms, particularly where the currency appreciation was large: in Malaysia, for example, wage costs in dollar terms rose by 68 per cent during 1990–1996 and in local currency by 33 per cent.[18] Growth in productivity and wages was associated with a rapid increase in employment; during the boom phase manufacturing employment rose by 43 per cent and 78 per cent in Malaysia and Thailand, respectively, and non-agricultural employment rose by 30 per cent in the Republic of Korea. Unemployment in all three countries practically disappeared, while it was moderate (under 5 per cent) in Indonesia (table 4.5).

By contrast, both the Latin American and Turkish booms were characterized by increases in real wages in excess of productivity (table 4.4).

Table 4.2

CHANGES IN MACROECONOMIC RATIOS OVER RECENT FINANCIAL CYCLES IN SELECTED LATIN AMERICAN COUNTRIES AND TURKEY

(Percentage points)

Country	Boom	Bust	Recovery
Argentina (1980s)	*(1979–1981)*	*(1982–1983)*	*(1984–1985)*
Savings	-8.5	2.0	-1.2
Investment	-5.1	-1.8	-3.3
Budget balance	-5.8	-1.3	2.4
Current-account balance	-9.2	3.7	1.3
Argentina (1990s)	*(1991–1994)*	*(1995–1996)*	*(1997–1998)*
Savings	-2.1	0.5	-0.7
Investment	5.9	-1.4	1.4
Budget balance	0.2	-1.9	0.6
Current-account balance	-6.8	2.3	-3.6
Chile	*(1978–1981)*	*(1982–1983)*	*(1984–1985)*
Savings	-3.2	0.2	7.1
Investment	2.4	-6.6	4.8
Budget balance	3.7	-5.2	0.3
Current-account balance	-10.4	8.6	-2.9
Mexico	*(1990–1994)*	*(1995–1996)*	*(1997–1998)*
Savings	-6.0	8.5	-3.0
Investment	-1.2	1.5	1.1
Budget balance	4.5	-0.2	-1.1
Current-account balance	-4.5	6.4	-3.3
Venezuela	*(1991–1993)*	*(1994–1996)*	*(1997–1998)*
Savings	-11.0	13.0	-12.0
Investment	5.9	-2.6	3.5
Budget balance	-2.3	3.7	-3.9
Current-account balance	-20.4	16.0	-15.5
Turkey	*(1990–1993)*	*(1994)*	*(1995–1997)*
Savings	0.0	0.5	-3.2
Investment	3.7	-1.9	0.5
Budget balance	-3.4	2.8	-4.8
Current-account balance	-4.4	6.5	-4.4

Source: World Bank, *Country at a Glance,* various issues (www.worldbank.org/data); ECLAC, *Preliminary Overview of the Economies of Latin America and the Caribbean,* various issues.

Note: The ratio of each variable to GDP in the last year of each phase is compared with that in the terminal year of the preceding phase.

In the Latin American episodes growth in labour productivity was relatively slow or even negative (e.g. Venezuela). Moreover, unlike in East Asia, unemployment kept on rising (see table 4.5), as in Argentina and Mexico (and also in Brazil), or stayed high, as in Chile and Venezuela. In addition, in Argentina, Brazil and Mexico rising wages were accompanied by declining levels of formal employment and increases in the labour force in the informal sector.[19]

The policy of reliance on capital inflows to support a consumption-led growth based, at least partly, on rising wages had a populist twist as it helped to correct some earlier distortions in income distribution at the expense of labour. Indeed,

Table 4.3

CHANGES IN REAL WAGES IN MANUFACTURING OVER RECENT FINANCIAL CYCLES IN SELECTED DEVELOPING COUNTRIES

(Per cent per annum[a])

Country	Boom	Bust	Recovery
Indonesia	5.6	-25.1	-
Malaysia	3.4	-1.2	n.a.
Republic of Korea	7.6	-4.9	13.9
Thailand	4.7	-2.3	3.2
Argentina (1980s)	4.1	-5.9	10.9
Argentina (1990s)	0.5	-0.5	-1.0
Chile	16.6	-3.3	-6.9
Mexico	6.2	-11.4	0.5
Venezuela	-3.5	-14.6	15.0
Turkey	16.1	-25.2	2.0

Source: UNCTAD secretariat estimates, based on ILO database (LABORSTA), http://laborsta.ilo.org/cgi-bin/broker.exe; ESCAP, *Economic and Social Survey of Asia and the Pacific 2000*, United Nations publication, sales no. E.00.II.F.19, New York, 2000; ECLAC, *Preliminary Overview of the Economies of Latin America and the Caribbean,* various issues.

Note: The periods of boom, bust and recovery are as defined in table 4.1.

a Change from the year immediately preceding the period in question to the last year of that period.

Table 4.4

INCREASE IN REAL WAGES AND LABOUR PRODUCTIVITY IN MANUFACTURING DURING RECENT PERIODS IN SELECTED DEVELOPING COUNTRIES

(Per cent[a])

Country	Period	Real wages	Labour productivity
Indonesia	(1990–1996)	46	85
Malaysia	(1991–1996)	22	34
Rep. of Korea	(1990–1996)	67	138
Thailand	(1988–1996)	32	32
Argentina	(1979–1981)	13	6
Chile	(1978–1981)	85	23
Mexico	(1990–1994)	35	22
Venezuela	(1991–1993)	-10	-11
Turkey	(1990–1993)	82	66

Source: See table 4.3.

a Percentage change from the year immediately preceding the boom period to the last year of that period.

Table 4.5

RATES OF UNEMPLOYMENT OVER RECENT FINANCIAL CYCLES IN SELECTED DEVELOPING COUNTRIES

(Per cent[a])

Country	Base	Boom	Bust	Recovery
Indonesia	2.5	4.7	5.5	6.4
Malaysia	5.1	2.5	4.9	4.5
Republic of Korea	2.6	2.0	6.8	6.3
Thailand	5.9	1.1	5.3	5.3
Argentina (1980s)	3.3	4.7	5.3	6.1
Argentina (1990s)	7.5	11.5	17.2	12.9
Chile	13.9	9.0	19.0	17.0
Mexico	2.9	3.7	5.5	3.2
Venezuela	10.4	6.6	11.8	11.2
Turkey	8.7	8.0	7.9	6.9

Source: See table 4.3.

a Unemployment in the last year of each of the phases in table 4.1 and in the year immediately preceding the boom ("base"), except for Indonesia, where the base refers to 1990.

most Latin American episodes and the Turkish boom had been preceded by a period of significant erosion of real wages. In Argentina the pre-boom real wage decline had been over 30 per cent in both episodes (1975–1978 and 1986–1989); it was 25 per cent in Brazil (1985–1991), over 40 per cent in Mexico (1984–1988) and Venezuela (1983–1990), and 33 per cent in Turkey (1979–1988). In all these cases there were also large declines in the share of wages in industrial value added.[20] By contrast, real wage reductions were not a feature of the pre-boom phase in East Asia, although there was some decline in Malaysia after the 1985 recession.

In most Latin American episodes, the pre-boom real wage erosion had taken place in an environment of chronic price instability, and the subsequent correction took place in the context of exchange-based stabilization programmes, often accompanied by rapid trade and financial liberalization. This populist policy mix thus served to avoid hard policy choices and allowed price stability to be achieved without running into distributional conflicts. However, in some cases, the correction turned out to be excessive, leading to real wage increases at the expense of profits. In Chile during the late 1970s, and in Brazil, Mexico, Turkey and Venezuela during the early and mid-1990s, rising real wages resulted in large declines in the share of profits. So long as the mass of profits was rising, this did not create a problem. However, since such wage-profit configurations depended on capital inflows, the rapid exit of capital and the decline in economic activity laid bare the latent conflicts, often leading to a redistribution from wages to profits.

2. The crisis

The effects of financial crises on key macroeconomic and labour market indicators depend, *inter alia*, on the evolution of these indicators during the boom phase. First, lower investment ratios during the crisis were generally a feature of countries which had experienced investment-led booms, as in East Asia and in Argentina in the 1990s. Declines in investment ratios were dramatic in the four Asian countries, exceeding 15 percentage points of GDP (table 4.1). On the other hand, the Latin American countries, which had consumption-led booms typically experienced sharp declines in consumption, reflected in rising private savings ratios (table 4.2). One exception was Chile in the early 1980s, where, despite a consumption-led boom, the burden of the subsequent adjustment in domestic absorption fell on investment.

Secondly, except in a few cases where the boom had been associated with rapidly rising public spending, the crises led to increases in public-sector deficits (tables 4.1 and 4.2). This was the case in East Asia as well as in many episodes in Latin America, where budgets turned from surpluses into deficits with the outbreak of the crisis. Of all the episodes considered here, it was only in Turkey and Venezuela that the ratio of the public deficit to GDP fell during the crisis. In most other cases where deficits rose, this was due to the effect of cyclical contraction on the budget rather than to discretionary fiscal expansion.

Third, in all cases the crisis led to a sharp turnaround in current-account balances (tables 4.1 and 4.2). In most Latin American countries this took the form of a sharp reduction in the current deficits, whereas in East Asia (as well as in Turkey and Venezuela) there was a shift from deficit to surplus. As a percentage of GDP, swings in the current-account balance often reached double-digit figures. Invariably, the shift was brought about by massive cuts in imports rather than export expansion.

Fourth, labour market conditions deteriorated in all countries with the outbreak of the financial crisis. Indeed, it appears that reduced incomes and employment in organized and informal labour markets have been the main social conduit of the adverse impact of financial crises on poverty and equality.[21] As in other episodes of emerging-market crisis, in East Asia too there was a sharp drop in the demand for urban labour. In 1998 manufacturing employment declined by 17 per cent in the Republic of Korea and 11 per cent in Indonesia, while construction employment fell by 37 per cent in Thailand. The surplus labour was partly absorbed elsewhere as workers crowded into low-wage jobs or self-employment in the urban informal sector, withdrew from the labour force, returned to the land,[22] engaged in part-time or unpaid family labour or, in the case of migrants, returned to their home country. Rising informalization and disguised unemployment appear to have been the trend almost everywhere.[23] In Indonesia the share of informal employment rose and – in contrast to other countries – the participation rate increased, suggesting that declines in wages brought down single-wage families below the poverty level. In the Republic of Korea, the ratio of temporary and daily workers (as opposed to regular employees) to total wage earners rose to 45 per cent in 1998 and 53 per cent in 1999.

Despite such flexibility and generally declining participation rates, unemployment rose everywhere (table 4.5). The sharpest rise was in the Republic of Korea, where the rate peaked at 8.7 per cent in February 1999, affecting particularly unskilled workers.[24] In Thailand it exceeded 5 per cent, whereas in Indonesia the increase continued throughout 1999, reaching 6.5 per cent in the first quarter of 2000. The unemployment rate in Malaysia doubled despite the repatriation of many migrant workers.

Falling real wages had a more serious social impact than rising unemployment in Indonesia and the Republic of Korea; in 1998 alone real wages fell by more than 40 per cent and 10 per cent, respectively. High inflation was the main cause in Indonesia and lower money wages in the Republic of Korea. Evidence from the latter country suggests that production workers, particularly in small- and medium-sized enterprises, were hit hardest by the crisis. Real wage declines appear to have been much more moderate in Malaysia and Thailand.[25]

Declines in wages and growing unemployment combined to produce a sharp increase in poverty throughout the region. In 1998 the number of people living on less than $1 a day was estimated at 65 million in the East Asian economies taken together, 10 million of whom were crisis-precipitated. These figures rise to 260 and 30 million, respectively, if the poverty benchmark is put at $2 a day.[26] Of these countries, poverty appears to have increased most in Indonesia and the Republic of Korea, a critical factor having been a faster increase in food prices than in prices of other consumer goods, particularly in Indonesia, where inflation accelerated rapidly.

The impact of financial crises on wages, employment and poverty was similar in earlier episodes in Latin America. In some cases the adjustment was more in terms of declines in real wages, which exceeded 20 per cent between the peak and the trough (e.g. in Mexico and Venezuela). The decline also exceeded 20 per cent in Turkey. In other Latin American episodes, wage declines were moderate but there were sharp increases in the unemployment rate, in the order of 6–10 percentage points, as in Argentina during 1995–1996 and in Chile during the Southern Cone crisis (table 4.5).

The impact on poverty in Latin America was equally devastating. Although growth during the first half of the 1990s had resulted in a gradual reduction of the high poverty levels inherited from the 1980s, even before the subsequent crises there were still more than 200 million living below the poverty line. One reason for the persistence of such high numbers was that growth in Latin America during the 1990s was generally accompanied by rising income inequalities. Taking into account the adverse impact of financial crises from the mid-1990s onwards, ECLAC estimated that the decade would end with higher levels of poverty than those of the 1980s.[27]

3. The recovery

The speed and sustainability of recovery from a financial crisis in an emerging market depends on how quickly the supply constraints of the economic downturn are overcome, the balance sheets of corporations and banks restructured, and new sources of demand exploited. On the supply side, perhaps the most important constraint arises from the breakdown of credit channels, both domestic and external. On the demand side, domestic private expenditure (both consumption and investment) is unlikely to play a major independent role in the recovery, which would have to rely on autonomous sources of demand, especially exports, which are typically stimulated by sharp currency depreciations. If allowed to operate, cyclical budget deficits can also act as built-in stabilizers.

As noted in the previous section, recovery is well under way in East Asia, even though at the end of 1999 incomes were still below the 1996 levels in Indonesia and Thailand. A comparison of investment ratios shows that, in all four countries, they are currently well below those attained during the peak, as well as below the levels attained before the boom in capital flows. As discussed in the subsequent section, investment ratios in these countries are unlikely to return to the peak levels even after the recovery is completed and productive capacities are fully utilized. In these respects the experience in Latin America was different. There, in most episodes where the boom was consumption-led, recovery in output was associated with a rise in the investment ratio. This was also the case in Turkey, where the boom in capital inflows was associated with fiscal expansion. In such cases, the post-crisis increases in investment often reflected the impact of currency realignment on profitability in the traded-good sectors.

In almost all episodes considered here, post-crisis savings ratios were higher than pre-crisis rates. The recovery in domestic savings was almost invariably due to a rise in private savings, since financial cycles typically lead to a deterioration in public finances. Indeed, except in Argentina during the Southern Cone crisis, post-crisis public-sector deficits were higher than pre-crisis deficits. An important reason is increased interest payments on public debt, which tend to mount during a crisis, partly as a result of higher interest rates and financial rescue operations. For instance, such payments in 1999 reached almost 4 per cent of GDP in Indonesia and absorbed as much as 30 per cent of tax revenues.[28]

Again, in all the episodes considered here, the domestic resource gap (the excess of investment over savings) was lower in the recovery phase than during the peak phase, as it was also in episodes where post-crisis investment was higher, with a consequent improvement in the current-account balance. Although, as recovery got under way, the trade balance started to move into deficit as imports picked up, the current-account balance always showed considerable improvement over the pre-crisis period. In East Asia, current accounts were still in surplus at the end of 1999, supporting reserve accumulation and debt repayments. However, in none of the Latin American episodes considered here did current accounts register a surplus during the crisis, let alone the recovery. Furthermore, post-crisis current-account deficits were much higher than before the surge in capital inflows, largely because of a deterioration in trade balances arising from rapid trade and financial liberalization.[29]

These shifts in macroeconomic aggregates, notably the narrowing of the domestic resource gap, as well as sharp currency devaluations over the financial cycle, suggest significant changes in income distribution. Indeed, they are often associated with declines in the share of wages in national income. In East Asia real wages have fully regained their pre-crisis level only in the Republic of Korea, while they remain depressed in Indonesia and Thailand. However, in all four countries, employment lagged considerably behind output. In the Republic of Korea at the end of 1999 GDP exceeded the pre-crisis level, but the unemployment rate was higher by more than 4 percentage points. There has been further improvement in the current year, but it appears to be due to declining participation rates; indeed, the World Bank has cautioned that unemployment rates might increase even if participation rates stabilize in the immediate future.[30] Again, in Malaysia GDP was about the same in 1999 as in the pre-crisis peak, but the unemployment rate was higher by 2 percentage points despite the shedding of migrant labour.

The same pattern is observed in almost all other episodes examined here. With the exception of the recovery in Argentina from the Southern Cone crisis, post-crisis real wages were lower than their peaks reached during the boom. Except for the Mexican cycle of the 1990s, this is also true for unemployment rates, which were higher in comparison not only with the peaks, but also with pre-boom levels. Further, for all cases where data are available, the share of wages in value added declined. Thus, the boom-bust-recovery cycles in both East Asia and Latin America appear to have been highly regressive so far as labour income is concerned.[31]

This deterioration in the conditions of labour, particularly among the unskilled, is a major reason why the reduction in poverty levels has so far lagged behind economic recovery in East Asia. Indeed, empirical studies show that there is a significant asymmetry in the impact of growth and crises on poverty in developing countries: the poverty-alleviating impact of a given rate of growth is significantly weaker than the poverty-augmenting impact of a comparable decline in GDP. In Indonesia and the Republic of Korea, improvements in headcount poverty indices, which had taken many years to achieve, were wiped out within a single year, and "returning to the pre-crisis level of poverty ... is likely to require more time ...".[32] According to the World Bank, under a "slow growth rising inequality" scenario associated with unfavourable global demand conditions, it would take East Asia over a decade to eliminate the poverty created by the financial crisis. Only with a return to a more "inclusive growth" strategy, where annual growth rates are closer to the long-term average for the region and inequality is unchanged, could the fight against poverty be effectively resumed.[33]

The persistence of widespread poverty and declines in wage incomes despite the recovery of output provide *prima facie* evidence that financial cycles result in regressive income distribution. However, it appears that for various reasons related to data problems as well as conceptual difficulties, the standard measures of income distribution cannot always capture such changes. In the Republic of Korea, for instance, the data show that while in the first quarter of 1995 the incomes of the richest 10 per cent were about 7 times those of the poorest 10 per cent, they were more than 10 times higher in the first quarter of 1999.[34] By contrast, Gini coefficients appear to have remained unchanged in Indonesia and Thailand, despite substantial increases in the poverty-stricken population in both countries.[35]

It is also extremely difficult to assess the equally important impact of financial crisis on wealth destruction, which appears to have hit primarily small- and medium-sized enterprises that provide extended family employment opportunities. The loss of income and employment in these sectors probably increases the share of population dependent on wage labour and brings an increase in formal unemployment. It may also contribute to the rise in saving ratios and explain the lag in consumption observed after the crisis as attempts are made to keep family-owned businesses alive.

D. Growth prospects and policy challenges

Despite rapid recovery, the concerns raised by the crisis in East Asia over growth prospects for the region have continued to dominate the policy debate. There is a growing opinion that structural and institutional weaknesses laid bare by the crisis need to be corrected, and that development strategies need to be adapted to the realities of globalization if the fight against poverty is to be effectively resumed and the gap with more advanced countries closed. Even then, it may not be possible to replicate the earlier growth performance; it will be necessary to settle for a growth path consistent with the logic of globalization. The financial crisis has, from this perspective, been a cathartic experience setting the stage for clearing away the institutional and policy vestiges of a bygone development era.[36]

The policy advice following from this perspective is clear: achieve much closer integration with the world economy, combined with institutional changes designed to reduce the risks associated with globalization. To that end reforms should aim at reduced state intervention, modernization of corporate and financial structures, deregulation of product and labour markets, and increased openness to foreign corporations, investment and trade. These measures follow from the diagnosis that the crisis occurred largely because government intervention and institutional practices had prevented firms and financial institutions from operating under the discipline of global market forces. Thus, greater openness and liberalization, rather than a retreat from globalization, holds the key to future success. Appropriate macroeconomic and exchange-rate policies, tighter prudential regulation and supervision of the financial system, and greater transparency and improved disclosure of macroeconomic variables, and of corporate and financial data, are essential ingredients of reforms to safeguard against the risks associated with closer integration with the world economy.

From this same perspective, the increased discipline of global market forces over national firms would also help overcome a major shortcoming of the East Asian process of accumulation and growth. The superior Asian performance in the past was based on exceptionally high savings and capital accumulation rather than on productivity growth. But this rapid pace of catch-up growth over the past few decades has been accompanied by excessive rent-seeking behaviour, lack of innovation, inefficient capital markets and institutional sclerosis, all of which have held total factor productivity (TFP) growth below potential. Greater competition brought about by institutional changes and closer integration into the world economy would help raise efficiency. This is all the more necessary in view of prospects of diminishing returns to capital accumulation, and of a tighter labour market that is likely to result from a lowering of what were relatively high participation rates.

According to an exercise undertaken by the World Bank, without faster TFP growth, output growth per capita associated with the same rate of investment in the next decade as in the 1990s is expected to decline by about 1.0 percentage points in the region. However, this could be more than offset by improvements in the macroeconomic, trade and financial spheres, and in public institutions, which could add as much as 2.0 percentage points in the Republic of Korea and Malaysia, 1.8 points in Thailand and 1.4 points in Indonesia.[37] Institutional reform and greater integration with the world economy are thus seen to constitute the basis of a new "miracle".

However, there seems to be considerable confusion regarding the past role of TFP in East Asia. Indeed, empirical estimates of its contribution to output growth fall within too wide a range to allow meaningful comparisons across countries and to draw firm conclusions for the future growth prospects of the region. For instance, while some studies found that during 1970–1985 developing countries such as Bangladesh, Cameroon, Congo, Pakistan and Uganda had higher TFP growth rates than the Republic of Korea and Taiwan Province of China,[38] the conclusion reached in an earlier World Bank study was totally different:

> What is most striking, however, is how little we are able to account for differences in growth rates between HPAEs [highly-performing Asian economies] and other economies on the basis of conventional economic variables ... Controlling for their superior rates of accumulation, the HPAEs still outperform, while sub-Saharan Africa and Latin America underperform the statistical relationship between accumulation and growth, leaving much of the regional difference in per capita income growth unexplained (even though a large fraction of HPAE success is explained). They have been apparently more successful in allocating the resources that they accumulated to high-productivity activities and in adopting and mastering catch-up technologies.[39]

A study undertaken in IMF gives yet different results regarding possible TFP growth in the East Asian countries. It finds that potential (feasible) TFP growth in the Republic of Korea is not much different from the rate attained during 1984–1994; it is moderately higher in Malaysia (0.5 per cent), substantially so in Indonesia (2.5 per cent), but lower in Thailand (0.7 per cent). Projections on this basis show a considerable slowdown in growth of per capita output in the Republic of Korea (to 4.0 per cent per annum) and Thailand

(4.9 per cent), little change for Malaysia (4.0 per cent), but an acceleration in Indonesia (6.0 per cent).[40] Clearly, these conflicting views regarding the past and potential TFP growth performance of East Asia, together with conceptual and empirical difficulties associated with this concept, cast serious doubts on the reliability of TFP growth as a guide to policy.

Given that hourly labour productivity in the Republic of Korea is around one half that of the major industrial countries, while in the second-tier NIEs it is much less, there is considerable scope in East Asia for productivity growth and technological catch-up based on structural change, but these are unlikely to come about without rapid investment. Investment and technical progress needed for catch-up growth might benefit from the pattern of regional aid, trade and FDI linkages which were instrumental to growth in East Asia in the 1980s and the early 1990s. In particular, high rates of investment and productivity growth based on a rapid increase in Japanese FDI in the region's information technology sector may play some role in restoring high growth rates.

However, as discussed in *TDR 1996*, the earlier regional growth dynamic hinged on a particular set of macroeconomic circumstances which promoted Japanese greenfield FDI in the region on an unprecedented scale along with a sharp rise in exports to Japan from Japanese affiliates. The resulting "hollowing out" of Japanese industry during the 1990s raises serious doubts about repeating the large outflows of FDI over the coming decade.[41] On the other hand, signs of a convergence in export structure among countries in the region pose the danger of heightened price competition, a tendency which is only likely to be exacerbated by the entry of new competitors from countries such as China and India.[42] Moreover, reliance on regional growth would, in view of the close links between trade and finance, call for more formal institutional arrangements to ensure the stability of financial markets. Equally important, prospects under such a scenario would still depend on robust growth and open markets in the North. In their absence, it is uncertain that there would be sufficient demand to absorb the increased output of IT goods from the region, even with an expansion in intraregional trade.

The financial crisis has shown that excessive reliance on external resources and markets leaves growth prospects in the region vulnerable to potentially sharp shocks and reversals in trade and finance, particularly when integration is not properly managed. Many of the institutions that functioned extremely well under a regime of strict control over international capital flows and investment decisions, including interlocking ownership between banks and non-bank corporations, the concentration of ownership in the hands of inside investors or high corporate leverage, became a source of instability with the dismantling of checks and balances and financial liberalization.[43] While altering these practices may result in undermining some positive entrepreneurial attitudes such as a vibrant corporate culture, a high animal spirit or taking a long view, such reforms would not necessarily guarantee financial stability even if they were accompanied by measures designed to increase disclosure and transparency and to strengthen prudential regulation and supervision of the financial system. The continuing incidence of financial instability and crises in industrial countries with state-of-the-art practices in these areas suggests that such reforms are unlikely to provide fail-safe protection.[44] The appropriate management of integration into the global financial system calls for measures that go beyond information disclosure and prudential regulations, and should include close supervision over private borrowing abroad, as well as tight control over speculative capital flows. As experience has shown, such forms of control are quite compatible with continued access to foreign capital.

Again, the events leading up to the crisis highlight the increased risk of vulnerability to trade shocks. While the emergence of new competitors in labour-intensive products was an important factor in the weakness of export performance for some of the second-tier NIEs, there was a sharp decline in the terms of trade for the first-tier NIEs between 1995 and 1997 which was, in part, due to excess capacity in higher technology sectors, such as semi-conductors.[45] Conditions were further complicated by the re-emergence of imbalances in global demand, the decline in developed country import propensities and instability in the yen-dollar exchange rate in the mid-1990s. These pressures culminated in a dramatic drop in the growth of manufacturing exports throughout the region in 1996 and 1997. Excess capacity continues to be particularly high in the second-tier NIEs and in key export sectors such as the automotive industry, where capacity utilization is as low as 40 per cent.[46] External demand prospects are also less favourable than in the past

because of global gluts in some key export sectors as more and more developing countries opt for export-led growth strategies. The cyclical boom in world semi-conductor prices which contributed significantly to the speed of recovery in some countries is expected to enter a downswing in 2002 due to heavy investments in that sector.

The increased vulnerability to trade shocks in manufactures results from far-reaching changes that have taken place in the global economy in the past few decades. International trade flows and prices have become more unstable partly because of increased instability of growth and persistent demand imbalances in the major industrial countries, and partly because of sharp swings in exchange rates and competitiveness. Moreover, as more and more developing countries opt for outward-oriented development strategies, the vulnerability to trade shocks and the risk of fallacy of composition have been increasing. In these respects today's conditions are quite different from those prevailing in the 1960s and 1970s, when only a handful of East Asian countries were pursuing outward-oriented strategies, had easy access to the markets of industrial countries, and faced no major challenge from other third-world producers or from the importing countries themselves. Indeed, the latter showed considerable tolerance of market penetration, thanks largely to cold-war politics.

In view of the increased vulnerability of rapid and inclusive growth to external trade and financial shocks, a more balanced long-term growth path may be desirable for countries in the region, reducing their dependence on foreign markets and resources.[47] In this respect conditions are different for first- and second-tier NIEs.

The Republic of Korea, where less than 10 per cent of the labour force is now in agriculture and per capita income is two thirds the Western European average, has entered a more demanding catch-up stage and is likely to face a rather different growth path from its neighbours in South-East Asia. Its position is similar to that of countries on the Western European periphery (Austria, Finland, Italy and Germany) in the early 1950s. Annual growth rates of some 5–6 per cent could still be expected over the coming two decades, down from some 8 per cent per annum during 1973–1992.[48] Domestic savings are high enough to bring this about without relying on foreign capital. Such a slowdown is to be expected with economic maturity; it occurred, for instance, in post-war Japan, where growth averaged some 8 per cent until the early 1970s, falling to 4 per cent thereafter, before collapsing in the 1990s. Regarding reliance on domestic and external markets, the post-1990 experience of Japan, as well as the post-war experience of Western Europe, hold useful lessons. The Japanese experience highlights the problems associated with heavy reliance on export-oriented industrial growth. Striking a more balanced growth path in the Republic of Korea is unlikely to require as extreme a shift as faced by Japan, since investment opportunities to strengthen competitiveness are still available, given the productivity gaps which exist with industrial economies. Even so, a strategy of greater reliance on domestic markets with stronger social dimensions, of the kind that underlined the successful experience of the Western European periphery during the Golden Age, offers a viable option. The elements of this experience are familiar: a rapid and parallel growth of real wages and productivity, strong growth in domestic demand, including rising public expenditures largely financed by taxation, and increased intraregional trade.[49] Emulation of this experience in the Republic of Korea should perhaps include a rise in the wage share, associated with a reduction in working hours, and an increase in public expenditure on health and education. Since the savings ratio was already very high prior to the crisis, and even allowing for a lower savings ratio over the coming decade as the wage share rises, there should be ample room to raise investment from the crisis levels without relying on foreign capital of the kind which distorted economic development prior to the crisis. A larger domestic market would also stimulate the wider adaptation of new information and telecommunications technologies, which appear to have high social returns. Although, this new investment dynamic would be consistent with closer regional ties, growth could actually be less dependent on foreign markets than in the past.

The position of the second-tier NIEs is somewhat different because the opportunities for catch-up are greater and their external linkages are likely to remain stronger. Their productivity gap with industrial countries is similar to the kind of gaps facing the first-tier NIEs in the early 1970s, and annual growth rates over the next two decades of some 7 per cent may not be unrealistic targets for these countries. At such low levels of income and labour productivity, they are unlikely to suffer from a rapidly diminishing return to capital, so that with a relatively high rate of accumulation they could attain considerable growth in labour productivity and per capita income. With domestic savings ratios over 30 per cent, heavy reliance on foreign savings would not be necessary. With abundant labour (much of it still employed in agriculture, where productivity levels are relatively low) and natural resources, there is considerable scope for structural change away from low-productivity sectors, which could lead to a considerable increase in overall labour productivity. New investment will be needed to upgrade manufacturing activities, including in more technology-intensive sectors, where import dependence is very high, and to ensure that a higher share of value-added from manufactured exports is retained in the domestic economy. In countries such as Malaysia, this would be consistent with a significant reduction in the share of imports in GDP as the domestic value-added content of exports increases. This healthier integration into the global trading system would also be consistent with an emphasis on capital formation in areas such as information infrastructure, transportation and training. Much of this investment would require rising public expenditures. Given the way in which high-tech sectors are organized internationally, industrial, trade and financial policies would be required that bring about the desired growth through a conscious effort by policy makers to direct and coordinate foreign and domestic investments and to develop local technological skills.[50] Thus, contrary to the mainstream view, renewing catch-up in the second-tier NIEs would still require the involvement of a developmental State, albeit with new, and in some respects even more demanding, policy agendas. ∎

Notes

1 Compare, for example, the actual growth rates for 1999 in table 2.1 above with the earlier projections given in table 1.4 of *TDR 1999*.

2 For a fuller analysis of the crisis see *TDR 1998, Part One*, chap. III; and for a more recent account see Akyüz Y, Causes and sources of the Asian financial crisis, paper presented at the Host Country Event: Symposium on Economic and Financial Recovery in Asia, UNCTAD X, Bangkok, 17 February 2000.

3 Ministry of Finance and Economy, the Republic of Korea's crisis resolution and its policy implications (final draft), G-20 Report, Seoul, December 1999: 18.

4 See Choi, Nakgyooon and Du-Yong Kang, A study on the crisis, recovery and industrial upgrading in the Republic of Korea, chapter eleven, in Divor-Frécaut D, Colaçon F and Hallward-Driemeier M, eds., *Asian Corporate Recovery. Findings from Firm-level Surveys in Five Countries*, Washington, DC, World Bank, April 2000.

5 For the case of Mexico see, e.g., *Safeguarding Prosperity in a Global Financial System: The Future International Financial Architecture*, Report of an Independent Task Force, Council on Foreign Relations, New York, November 1999: 31 (www.foreignrelations.org/public/pubs/IFA Task-Force.htm).

6 This collateral effect was subsequently recognized by IMF: "These [trade and current account] surpluses will help countries to reconstitute their depleted foreign exchange reserves and thereby restore the confidence of investors in the ability of the authorities to meet normal demands for foreign exchange" (IMF, *World Economic Outlook*, Oct. 1998: 38).

7 For a summary of changes in the contents of the IMF programme during 1997–1998 see Ha-Joon Chang and Chul-Gyue Yoo, The triumph of the rentiers: The 1997 Korean crisis in a historical perspective, Paper presented at the Workshops on the World Financial Authority, Centre for Economic Policy Analysis, New School University, New York, 6–7 July and 20–21 November 1999, table 3.

8 For a relatively up-to-date account of the evolution of various macroeconomic variables in the East Asian recovery process see Asian Development Bank, *Asia Recovery Report: May Update*, Manila, May 2000. Unless otherwise stated, the figures for various policy and performance indicators used here are from that source.

9 According to a survey among Korean firms, local lenders were considered even more restrictive than foreign banks (Choi and Kang, op. cit.: 17).

10 IMF, op. cit.: 41–42.

11 See *OECD Economic Outlook*, Dec. 1999: 96.

12 IMF News Brief No. 00/27, IMF completes final review of Thai Program, 8 May 2000.

13 IMF, *World Economic Outlook*, Oct. 1999, table 2.7. It was not, however, indicated to what extent the expected recovery in private investment would come from a replenishment of inventories and to what extent from fixed capital formation.

14 Most of these episodes were examined in past issues of *TDR*. For the crisis in the Southern Cone see *TDR 1998*, Part One, annex to chapter III; in Mexico and Argentina in 1994–1995, see *TDR 1995*, Part Two, chap. II; see also the discussion of the Brazilian crisis in *TDR 1999*, chap. III.

15 See *TDR 1998*, Part One, chap. III.

16 The date of the beginning of the cycle (the base period) does not change whether one uses net capital inflows (that is, net acquisition of domestic assets by non-residents) or net flows (inclusive of net acquisition of foreign assets by residents). For the definition of these concepts see *TDR 1999*, box 5.1.

17 ECLAC, *Equity, Development and Citizenship*, LC/G.2071(SES.28/3), Santiago, Chile, March 2000: 224.

18 During the boom phase of the cycle it was only in the Republic of Korea, among these four countries, that the divergence between the growth rates of the dollar wages and real wage costs (i.e. nominal wages deflated by the index of wholesale prices) was not large; the cumulative increases from the base to the peak were 114 and 104 per cent, respectively. The corresponding figures were 59 per cent and 44 per cent in Indonesia, and 117 per cent and 34 per cent in Thailand.

19 Industrial employment declined during 1992–1994 in Argentina and 1990–1994 in Brazil and Mexico, while the share of informal employment rose in all three countries; see Amadeo EJ, The knife-edge of exchange-rate-based stabilization: Impact on growth, employment and wages, *UNCTAD Review 1996*, United Nations publication, sales no. E.97.II.D.2, New York and Geneva, 1996. Using a broad sectoral classification, ECLAC estimates that urban informal employment rose from 44 per cent of the total in 1990 to 58 per cent in 1998 (ECLAC,

op. cit., figure 5.1). According to ILO data, manufacturing employment declined by 5 per cent and 8 per cent during the early 1990s in Argentina and Mexico, respectively, and by 10 per cent from 1990 to 1997 in Brazil.

20 In Chile, on the other hand, real wages were on an upward trend from 1975 onwards, but the immediate post-Allende data are not available.

21 This view is shared in almost all recent World Bank publications on the East Asian crisis. See also Diwan I, Labor shares and financial crises (preliminary draft), Washington, DC, World Bank, November 1999. By contrast, according to another study, "incomes of the poor do not fall more than proportionately during economic crises"; see Dollar D and Kraay A, Growth is good for the poor (preliminary draft), March 2000 (www.worldbank.org/research). Studies on income distribution by the UNCTAD secretariat show that the economic crisis beginning in the early 1980s was associated with a rise in the share of the top 20 per cent at the expense of middle classes rather than the poorest 20 per cent. It was also noted that crises could generate a process of "equalizing downwards" in rural economies in Africa, but it is not clear if such results could be generalized to emerging markets facing sharp declines in output due to financial crises; see *TDR 1997*, Part Two, chap. III.

22 However, with the exception of Indonesia, agriculture provided little buffer; see Poapongsakorn N, Agriculture as a source of recovery?, Bangkok, Thailand Development Research Institute, 1999; and World Bank, *Global Economic Prospects and the Developing Countries 2000*, Washington, DC, Dec. 1999: 54.

23 See Asian Development Bank, *Asian Development Outlook 2000*, Manila, 2000: 51; World Bank, *East Asia: Recovery and Beyond*, Washington, DC, 2000: 117–119; and Clerissi G, L'impact de la crise sur le marché du travail en Thaïlande, mimeo (Les Notes des Postes d'Expansion Économique), Bangkok, Nov. 1998.

24 Data of the National Statistical Office of the Republic of Korea. See also Jong-Il You and Ju-Ho Lee, Economic and social consequences of globalization: The case of South Korea, Working Paper no. 17, New York, Centre for Economic Policy Analysis, New School University, February 2000. Although the official unemployment figure in the Republic of Korea for mid-1999 was around 1.5 million, the Korean Confederation of Trade Unions (KCTU) puts it at 4 million, taking into account workers discouraged from seeking employment.

25 These estimates are from World Bank, *Global Economic Prospects and the Developing Countries 2000*, Dec. 1999, table 2.2. Different estimates for Thailand are given, for example, by Siamwalla A and Sobchokchai O (*Responding to the Thai Crisis*, UNDP Working Paper, Bangkok, May 1998).

26 World Bank, op. cit, table 1.8a. See also World Bank, *East Asia: Recovery and Beyond*, table 1.2.

27 ECLAC, op. cit.: 66. The number of households living below the poverty line in Latin America rose from 35 per cent to 41 per cent from 1980 to 1990, rising in all countries except Chile (ECLAC, *The Equity Gap, Latin America, the Caribbean and the South Summit*, LC/G.1954(CONF.86/3), Santiago, Chile, March 1997, table 1.2). The ratio had declined during 1990–1997, but at 36 per cent it was higher in 1997 than in 1980. During this period the share of the poor rose in both Mexico and Venezuela. On the other hand, in 13 Latin American countries for which data for the same period are available, the Gini coefficient rose in nine and declined in four (ECLAC, *Equity, Development and Citizenship*, March 2000, chap. 2, sect. 3(c)).

28 World Bank, *East Asia: Recovery and Beyond*, 2000, table 5.1 and figure 5.2.

29 See *TDR 1999*, chap. IV.

30 World Bank, *East Asia: From Recovery to Sustained Growth. An Update*, March 2000. The persistence of a high rate of employment despite recovery has been explained, in part, by policy measures to increase the degree of labour market flexibility (Asian Development Bank, *Asian Development Outlook 2000*: 50–51).

31 For a similar conclusion, see Diwan, op. cit.

32 World Bank, *Global Economic Prospects and the Developing Countries 2000*: 54.

33 Under the Bank's first scenario, per capita income growth would reach 4.0 per cent per annum, but inequality would increase by 10 per cent, and there would still be 58.3 million people in East Asia living below $1 per day in 2008, compared with 55.1 million in 1998 (ibid.: 28–36). "Inclusive growth" assumes an annual per capita growth rate of 4.9 per cent, compared to actual growth in East Asia of 5.2 per cent per annum in 1965–1973, 4.7 per cent in 1973–1980 and 6.3 per cent in 1980–1989. On this basis, the World Bank estimates that 18 million people would still be living on less than $1 a day by 2008.

34 Chang and Yoo, op. cit.: 32–33.

35 One explanation is the fact that household surveys on income disregard relative price changes in countries (such as Indonesia) where the poor faced significantly higher inflation than the rich. Another is that household surveys undertaken in 1998 included questions about household incomes during the preceding year (i.e. 1997) and therefore failed to capture the full impact of the crisis. On these empirical issues, see World Bank, *East Asia: Recovery and Beyond*, 2000:114-116.

36 See Crafts N, *East Asian Growth Before and After the Crisis*, IMF Working Paper, WP/98/137, Washington, DC, Sept. 1998; IMF, *World Economic Outlook*, Oct. 1998, chap. III; and World Bank, *East Asia: Recovery and Beyond*, op. cit., chap. 7.

37 World Bank, op. cit.: 144–146.

38 On various empirical estimates of TFP growth see Singh A, The causes of fast economic growth in East Asia, *UNCTAD Review 1995*, United Nations

publication, sales no. E.95.II.D.23, New York and Geneva, 1995: 95–99; and Crafts, op. cit.

39   World Bank, *The East Asian Miracle,* New York, Oxford University Press for the World Bank, 1993: 54.

40   Crafts, op. cit., particularly tables 11 and 14.

41   See Akyüz Y, New trends in Japanese FDI: Postindustrial transformation and policy challenges, in Kozul-Wright R and Rowthorn R, eds., *Transnational Corporations and the Global Economy,* London, Macmillan, 1998.

42   See World Bank, op. cit.: 52–53.

43   See *TDR 1998*, Part One, chap. III; and Akyüz Y, Causes and sources of the Asian financial crisis, paper presented at the Host Country Event: Symposium on Economic and Financial Recovery in Asia, UNCTAD X, Bangkok, 17 February 2000, and the references therein.

44   For a discussion of these issues see Akyüz Y and Cornford A, Capital flows to developing countries and the reform of the international financial system", UNCTAD *Discussion Paper*, no. 143, Geneva, Nov. 1999.

45   For a discussion of some of these pressures, see *TDR 1996*, Part Two, chap. II; Bank for International Settlements, *68th Annual Report*, Basle, 1998: 33–38; Grilli E, The Asian crisis: Trade and trade policy consequences, Buenos Aires, Latin American Trade Network, FLACSO, 1999; Maizels A et al., The manufactures terms of trade of developing countries with the United States 1981–97 (mimeo), Queen Elizabeth House, University of Oxford, March 2000. On the specific details of the Korean electronics sector see Kaplinsky R, 'If you want to get somewhere else, you must run at least twice as fast as

that!' The roots of the East Asian crisis (mimeo), Institute of Development Studies, University of Sussex, Brighton, United Kingdom, June 1998.

46   See Asian Development Bank, op. cit.: 4; and JP Morgan, Savings and investment in the crisis economies, *Global Data Watch*, 28 April 2000. Excess capacity also remains a serious problem in some non-tradeable sectors such as real estate, which contributed up to half of overall fixed investment prior to the crisis.

47   See also ESCAP, *Economic and Social Survey of Asia and the Pacific 1998*, United Nations publication, sales no. E.98.II.F.59, Bangkok, 1998; Islam A, The dynamics of Asian crisis and selected policy implications, in Herman B, ed., *Global Financial Turmoil and Reform. A United Nations Perspective*, United Nations publication, sales no. E.99.III.A.8, Tokyo, United Nations University Press, 1999.

48   In Austria, Finland and Italy GDP per hour worked in 1950 stood at around 45 per cent and in the (then) Federal Republic of Germany at around 50 per cent that of Switzerland, the lead European economy in that year. Annual per capita real GDP growth rates in 1950–1973 were between 4 and 5 per cent.

49   See Marglin S and Schor J, eds., *The Golden Age of Capitalism: Reinterpreting the Postwar Experience*, Oxford, Clarendon Press, 1990.

50   See Lowe N and Kennedy M, Foreign investment and the geography of production: Why the Mexican consumer electronics industry failed, *World Development*, 27(8), 1999; Ostry S and Gestrin M, Foreign direct investment, technology transfer and the innovation-network model, *Transnational Corporations*, 2(3), Dec. 1993; and *TDR 1996*, Part Two, chap. II.

UNITED NATIONS CONFERENCE ON TRADE AND DEVELOPMENT

Palais des Nations
CH-1211 GENEVA 10
Switzerland
(http://www.unctad.org)

Selected UNCTAD Publications

Trade and Development Report, 1998 United Nations publication, sales no. E.98.II.D.6
ISBN 92-1-112427-1

Part One International Financial Instability and the World Economy

  I The World Economy: Performance and Prospects
  II Trade Implications of the East Asian Crisis
    Annex: Impact of the Asian Crisis on Specific commodities
  III International Financial Instability and the East Asian Crisis
    Annex: Three Post-Bretton Woods Episodes of Financial Crisis
  IV The Management and Prevention of Financial Crises

Part Two African Development in a Comparative Perspective

  Introduction
  I Growth and Development in Africa: Trends and Prospects
  II The Role, Structure and Performance of Agriculture
  III Agricultural Policies, Prices and Production
  IV Trade, Accumulation and Industry
  V Policy Challenges and Institutional Reform

Trade and Development Report, 1999 United Nations publication, sales no. E.99.II.D.1
ISBN 92-1-112438-7

Part One The World Economy: Fragile Recovery with Downside Risks

  I The World Economy: Performance and Prospects
  II International Trade and the Trading System
  III International Financial Markets: Instability, Trends and Prospects

Part Two Trade, External Financing and Economic Growth in Developing Countries

  Introduction
  IV Payments Deficits, Liberalization and Growth in Developing Countries
    Annex: Trade deficits, liberalization and growth in developing countries:
        Some econometric estimates
  V Capital Flows to Developing Countries
  VI Rethinking Policies for Development

International Monetary and
Financial Issues for the 1990s

Volume X (1999)   United Nations publication, sales no. E.99.II.D.14
ISBN 92-1-112453-0

Andrew Cornford and Jim Brandon
The WTO Agreement on Financial Services: Problems of Financial Globalization in Practice
A.V. Ganesan
Strategic Options Available to Developing Countries with Regard to a
Multilateral Agreement on Investment
Carlos M. Correa
Key Issues for Developing Countries in a Possible Multilateral Agreement on Investment
Manuel R. Agosin
Capital-Account Convertibility and Multilateral Investment Agreements:
What is in the Interest of Developing Countries?
Christian Larraín
Banking supervision in developing economies
Percy S. Mistry
Coping with Financial Crises: Are Regional Arrangements the Missing Link?
Devesh Kapur
The World Bank's Net Income and Reserves: Sources and Allocation
Lance Taylor
Lax Public Sector, Destabilizing Private Sector: Origins of Capital Market Crises
Paul Mosley
Globalization, Economic Policy and Growth Performance

Volume XI* (1999)   United Nations publication, sales no. E.99.II.D.25
ISBN 92-1-112465-4

Montek S. Ahluwalia
The IMF and the World Bank in the New Financial Architecture
Stephany Griffith-Jones with Jenny Kimmis
The BIS and its Role in International Financial Governance
Aziz Ali Mohammed
Adequacy of International Liquidity in the Current Financial Environment
Steven Radelet
Orderly Workouts for Cross-border Private Debt
Andrew Cornford
Standards for Transparency and Banking Regulation and Supervision: Contrasts and Potential
William Milberg
Foreign Direct Investment and Development: Balancing Costs and Benefits
Kwesi Botchwey
Country Ownership and Development Cooperation: Issues and the Way Forward
Giovanni Andrea Cornia
Social Funds in Stabilization and Adjustment Programmes
Bhagirath Lal Das
Strengthening Developing Countries in the WTO

---

*   This volume concludes the series *International Monetary and Financial Issues for the 1990s*, published in the context of the
UNCTAD Project of Technical Support to the Intergovernmental Group of Twenty-Four on International Monetary Affairs.
As of the year 2000, the studies prepared under this project are published individually, jointly by UNCTAD and Harvard
University, in a new series entitled *G-24 Discussion Paper Series.*

✱✱✱✱✱✱

These publications may be obtained from bookstores and distributors throughout the world. Consult your bookstore
or write to United Nations Publications/Sales Section, Palais des Nations, CH-1211 Geneva 10, Switzerland
(Fax: +41-22-917.0027; E-mail: unpubli@un.org; Internet: www.un.org/publications); or from United Nations
Publications, Two UN Plaza, Room DC2-853, Dept. PERS, New York, NY 10017, USA (Tel. +1-212-963.8302 or
+1-800-253.9646; Fax +1-212-963.3489; E-mail: publications@un.org).

G-24 Discussion Paper Series

Research papers for the Intergovernmental
Group of Twenty-Four on International Monetary Affairs

No. 1	March 2000	Arvind PANAGARIYA	The Millennium Round and Developing Countries: Negotiating Strategies and Areas of Benefits
No. 2	May 2000	T. Ademola OYEJIDE	Interests and Options of Developing and Least-developed Countries in a New Round of Multilateral Trade Negotiations
No. 3	May 2000	Andrew CORNFORD	The Basle Committee's Proposals for Revised Capital Standards: Rationale, Design and Possible Incidence
No. 4	June 2000	Katharina PISTOR	The Standardization of Law and Its Effect on Developing Economies
No. 5	June 2000	Andrés VELASCO	Exchange-rate Policies for Developing Countries: What Have We Learned? What Do We Still Not Know?
No. 6	August 2000	Devesh KAPUR and Richard WEBB	Governance-related Conditionalities of the International Financial Institutions

******

G-24 Discussion Paper Series are available on the website at: www.unctad.org/en/pub/pubframe.htm. Copies may be obtained from the Editorial Assistant, Macroeconomic and Development Policies, Division on Globalization and Development Strategies, United Nations Conference on Trade and Development (UNCTAD), Palais des Nations, CH-1211 Geneva 10, Switzerland (Tel. +41-22-907.5733; Fax +41-22-907.0274; E-mail: nicole.winch@unctad.org).

African Development in a Comparative Perspective

Published for and on behalf of the United Nations

United Nations sales no. GV.E.99.0.21

ISBN 92-1-101004-7 (United Nations)

Introduction
I   Growth and Development in Africa: Trends and Prospects
II   The Role, Structure and Performance of Agriculture
III   Agricultural Policies, Prices and Production
IV   Trade, Accumulation and Industry
V   Policy Challenges and Institutional Reform

******

This publication may be obtained from United Nations Publications/Sales Section, Palais des Nations, CH-1211 Geneva 10, Switzerland (Fax: +41-22-917.0027; E-mail: unpubli@un.org; Internet: www.un.org/publications); or from James Currey Ltd, 73 Botley Road, Oxford OX2 0BS, UK; or from Africa World Press, P.O. Box 1892 Trenton NJ 08607, USA.

UNCTAD Discussion Papers

No. 130, March 1998	Matti VAINIO	The effect of unclear property rights on environmental degradation and increase in poverty
No. 131, Feb./March 1998	Robert ROWTHORN & Richard KOZUL-WRIGHT	Globalization and economic convergence: An assessment
No. 132, March 1998	Martin BROWNBRIDGE	The causes of financial distress in local banks in Africa and implications for prudential policy
No. 133, March 1998	Rubens LOPES BRAGA	Expanding developing countries' exports in a global economy: The need to emulate the strategies used by transnational corporations for international business development
No. 134, April 1998	A.V. GANESAN	Strategic options available to developing countries with regard to a Multilateral Agreement on Investment
No. 135, May 1998	Jene K. KWON	The East Asian model: An explanation of rapid economic growth in the Republic of Korea and Taiwan Province of China
No. 136, June 1998	JOMO K.S. & M. ROCK	Economic diversification and primary commodity processing in the second-tier South-East Asian newly industrializing countries
No. 137, June 1998	Rajah RASIAH	The export manufacturing experience of Indonesia, Malaysia and Thailand: Lessons for Africa
No. 138, October 1998	Z. KOZUL-WRIGHT & Lloyds STANBURY	Becoming a globally competitive player: The case of the music industry in Jamaica
No. 139, December 1998	Mehdi SHAFAEDDIN	How did developed countries industrialize? The history of trade and industrial policy: The cases of Great Britain and the USA
No. 140, February 1999	M. BRANCHI, A. GABRIELE & V. SPIEZIA	Traditional agricultural exports, external dependency and domestic prices policies: African coffee exports in a comparative perspective
No. 141, May 1999	Lorenza JACHIA & Ethél TELJEUR	Free trade between South Africa and the European Union – A quantitative analysis
No. 142, October 1999	J. François OUTREVILLE	Financial development, human capital and political stability
No. 143, November 1999	Yilmaz AKYÜZ & Andrew CORNFORD	Capital flows to developing countries and the reform of the international financial system
No. 144, December 1999	Wei GE	The dynamics of export-processing zones
No. 145, January 2000	B. ANDERSEN, Z. KOZUL-WRIGHT & R. KOZUL-WRIGHT	Copyrights, competition and development: The case of the music industry
No. 146, February 2000	Manuel R. AGOSIN & Ricardo MAYER	Foreign investment in developing countries: Does it crowd in domestic investment?
No. 147, April 2000	Martin KHOR	Globalization and the South: Some critical issues
No. 148, April 2000	Yilmaz AKYÜZ	The debate on the international financial architecture: Reforming the reformers
No. 149, July 2000	Mehdi SHAFAEDDIN	What did Frederick List actually say? Some clarifications on the infant industry argument
No. 150, August 2000	Jörg MAYER	Globalization, technology transfer and skill accumulation in low-income countries

******

Copies of **UNCTAD Discussion Papers** may be obtained from the Editorial Assistant, Macroeconomic and Development Policies, GDS, UNCTAD, Palais des Nations, CH-1211 Geneva 10, Switzerland (Tel. 41-22-907.5733; Fax 41-22-907.0274; E-mail: nicole.winch@unctad.org). The full texts of *UNCTAD Discussion Papers* from No. 140 onwards, as well as abstracts of earlier ones, are available on the UNCTAD website at: www.unctad.org/en/pub/pubframe.htm.